From

The Women
34 Great Sutton Stree

Jean Stead   Photo: Debbie Rogers

Jean Stead is a former news editor of the *Guardian* and has
been its Scottish Correspondent for the past four years. She
covered the miners' strike in Scotland for her paper, during
which time she also wrote on the women's support groups.

    She previously specialised as a writer on the nuclear
disarmament issue internationally. She wrote the first articles
in the *Guardian* about the Greenham Common women's
peace camp, and on the rise of the German Greens Party.
Her special features have included series on the police, the
law and the right to protest.

JEAN STEAD

Never the Same Again

Women and the Miners' Strike 1984–85

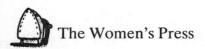 The Women's Press

First published by The Women's Press Limited 1987
A member of the Namara Group
34 Great Sutton Street, London EC1V 0DX

Copyright © Jean Stead 1987
All rights reserved

British Library Cataloguing in Publication Data

Stead, Jean
    Never the Same aGain
    1. Strikes and lockouts—Miners—Great Britain—
    History—20th century   2. Women—Great Britain—
    History—20th century
    I. Title
    305.4'890694   HD5365.M6

    ISBN 0-7043-3983-8

Typeset by MC Typeset Limited, Chatham, Kent
Printed and bound in Great Britain by
Hazell Watson & Viney Ltd, Aylesbury, Bucks.

To women and men of
Polmaise Colliery

Contents

Acknowledgements   viii

Chronology of the Strike   ix
Introduction   1

1   Headlong into Politics   10
    *Coming Together – Education – Public Speaking – Support
    Groups – The Barnsley March – The National Women's
    Organisation – Women Against Pit Closures – International
    Politics – Women and the Labour Party – Exploitation of the
    Women – A Working-Class Women's Movement*

2   Something Else in the House   31
    *Fund Raising – The Soup Kitchens – Food Parcels – Changing
    Roles – Family Upheavals*

3   Coal and Greenham Common   47
    *The Edinburgh Gala – Support from Greenham – Visits to
    Greenham – Greenham Women and the Miners – Carry
    Greenham Home*

4   On the Picket Line   59
    *Police Tactics – Hatfield Main – Women and the Violence –
    Armethorpe Colliery – Grimethorpe Colliery – The Media and
    NUM Reaction – The Picketing Continues – Monktonhall
    Colliery – Polkemmet Colliery – Emley Moor Colliery – Links
    with other Industries*

5   Militant Solidarity   79
    Maerdy – Kent

6 The Eye of the Storm 95

*Isolation – The Clipstone Soup Kitchen – Blidworth Colliery –
NCB Propaganda – Violence and the Police – Family Divisions
– Miners' Wives and Minority Groups – Nottinghamshire
Women and the Barnsley March – A Fight for the Future*

7 Changing Relationships 112

*Women and the NUM – The Eppleton Area Miners' Wives'
Support Group – The Walking Wounded*

8 The Miners Come to Town 130

*Support from London – Support from other Areas – Not Just
Tea and Sandwiches – Public Support – Trade Union Support –
The Christmas Appeal – The NCB Backlash – The February
Appeal*

9 Winter 141

*The Cold – The Lack of Food – The Derbyshire Women's
Action Group – The Barnsley Women Against Pit Closures –
Christmas 1984 – The Beginning of the End*

10 The End of the Strike 153

*The Return to Work – The End of the Strike and the End of
Maerdy – Their Heads Held High*

11 Never the Same Again 160

Colliery Closures 1985–87 169

Index 171

Acknowledgments

With additional research by Indra de Lanerolle.

   With acknowledgments to John Bourne and Maggie
Conlin; Betty Heathfield, Jean Miller, Ella Egan, Calum
MacIntosh, Hilary Wainwright, Kate Bennett, Paul
Hoyland, Vic Allen, Malcolm Pithers, Rebecca Johnson,
Anne Suddick, Sarah Hipperson, John McCormack; and the
miners and women at Polmaise colliery, and at Monktonhall,
Bilston Glen, Snowdown, Hatfield Main, Ollerton,
Clipstone, Maerdy, Cardowan, the pits of the Dulais valley,
South Wales, Woolley, and other Yorkshire pits, Easington
and Eppleton, and strike centres in every coalfield in Britain;
and to Loulou Brown, my editor.

Chronology of the Strike

February 1984: Polmaise colliery closure announced, overtime banned in Scotland, over 4000 miners strike.

March 1984: National Coal Board announces closure of Cortonwood colliery and cutback of 4 million tonnes of coal in the forthcoming year, with a loss of 20 000 jobs.

Miners' strike begins, March 9.

First women's group meets in Barnsley, sets up Women in Support of Miners. Letter setting out opposition to closure sent to local press.

David Jones killed while picketing at Ollerton in Yorkshire, March 15. Kent miners on their way to picket stopped by police and turned back at Dartford tunnel.

Lancashire miners join strike.

Barnsley Women Against Pit Closures formed. They organise picket at Grimethorpe NCB headquarters. NUM executive split on whether or not to hold a ballot.

April 1984: NUM exectuive at Sheffield changes rules so that only 50% vote is needed to decide on strike action. Special delegate conference in Sheffield endorses NEC decision and ratifies strike action 'in accordance with rule 41'.

Barnsley Women Against Pit Closures decide (April 22) to hold a national women's rally and march through Barnsley on May 12.

May 1984: 3 men injured and 65 arrested at Ravenscraig steel works (May 8) when mounted police break up the miners' picket line. Scottish miners' leaders press railway workers to stop carrying iron ore for the steel plant from the Scottish port of Hunterston.

Barnsley Women Against Pit Closures launches women's march, with delegates from coalfields all over Britain. Arthur Scargill leads the march and speaks on the platform at the Civic Hall rally (May 12).

In Mansfield, Notts, 40 000 people march in support of the strike (May 14).

Anne Scargill is arrested at Silverhill colliery (May 16).

Leon Brittain, Home Secretary, admits that plain-clothes police are operating in Nottinghamshire to protect working miners.

First meeting since the strike began takes place between the national union and the coal board (May 23), and breaks up in less than half an hour.

5000 picket Orgreave coking plant: 82 are arrested, including Arthur Scargill, and 62 injured (May 30).

Approx. 3200 police, some in riot gear, from 13 forces, are drafted into Orgreave.

June 1984: Two convoys of lorries meet 3000 pickets at Orgreave. Nineteen arrested, 20 people injured, including 5 police officers (June 1).

First House of Commons debate on the strike. 12 000 miners and supporters march from Kings Cross to Westminster, 100 are arrested (June 7).

Bruce Kent, CND leader, addresses Scottish Miners' Gala at Edinburgh (June 9).

Joe Green, miner, is crushed to death by a lorry while on picket duty at Ferrybridge (June 15).

10 000 pickets turn out at Orgreave, 93 are arrested, Arthur Scargill is injured (June 18).

Kent Women's Demonstration (June 23).

Jean McCrindle writes to the *Sunday Times* proposing an NUM Associate Membership for women.

July 1984: Home Secretary endorses use of criminal rather than civil law against miners.

NUM and NCB talks last nine hours, with agreement to meet again (July 5).

Government withholds estimated £6.8 million in tax refunds due to striking miners (July 13).

Court appearance of 10 Barnsley Women Against Pit Closures arrested on picket line (July 13).

First National Women Against Pit Closures conference held at Northern College, Barnsley (July 22).

August 1984: National Women Against Pit Closures rally in London. A petition handed to the Queen (August 11).

Miners drifting back to work, but slowly.

Forty arrested when 3000 pickets cover five pits that have reopened (August 21).

Second dock strike called, following unloading of coal from coke ship *Ostia* by British Steel workers at Hunterston (August 24).

Action at Port Talbot steelworks – 100 South Wales miners occupy 3 cranes 120 feet high (August 31).

Sit-down protest at Hatfield Main in Yorkshire (August 31).

Striking miners visit Greenham Common peace camp throughout the month.

September 1984: Mass picket of 3500 at Kiverton Park. Three-week-old National Dock Strike called off (September 18).

Bishop of Durham calls for Ian MacGregor's resignation. At one Scottish meeting MacGregor arrives with a green plastic bag over his head.

NCB avoids strike by NACODS union, responsible for safety cover in the pits, by offering them a compromise package (September 26).

October 1984: Costs of strike now estimated at £600 million.

Unemployment figures reach 3284 million – 13.6% of national work force (October 5).

NUM and NCB agree to meet with ACAS as chair (October 8).

Twenty-two people arrested for coal picking in Grimethorpe (October 14).

Greenham Common women donate food to Women Against Pit Closures.

Deadline expires for NUM to pay £200 000 fine and court attempts to seize NUM funds (October 25).

Strike threatened by NACODS called off by executive after accepting NCB proposals.

Coal stocks at power stations down – only 4–10 weeks' supply at Ferrybridge (October 29).

NCB offers miners a back-to-work bonus. Christmas appeals for miners' families start.

November 1984: Mines Not Missiles rally held in York (November 3).

NCB claims drift back to work a success, but Arthur Scargill says strike still solid (November 6).

Dublin court rules £2.7 million NUM funds to be frozen (November 7).

It is announced tht only £8 174 of an estimated £10.6 million NUM funds are in the hands of the sequestrators (November 9).

National Conference of Women's Action Groups at Chesterfield (November 10–11).

1900 return to work. Mass picket at Cortonwood (November 12).

Benefit concert held in London (November 25). First meeting to form Barnsley's second, alternative, women's group. Visit by Barnsley women to Greenham Common, with WAPC members from other areas.

David Wilkie is killed by a concrete block smashed through the roof of his minicab (November 30).

December 1984: Ian MacGregor speaks in favour of privatising the pits (December 5).

Toys start to arrive for miners' children for Christmas:

from I G Metal in Germany; three lorry-loads from Belgium; £100 000 worth of toys from France. Children also go abroad for Christmas holidays in Europe.

The national Christmas appeal for miners and their families is published in the British press.

January 1985: Mass picketing continues at Yorkshire Main and Grimethorpe collieries, and at Kiverton Park.

Return to work continues only slowly.

Challenge in High Court to government's right to deduct £16 from supplementary benefits paid to miners' families fails (January 22).

Energy Secretary refuses Welsh Church leaders' request to hold independent enquiry into the future of the coal industry.

Peter Heathfield, NUM general secretary, meets NCB industrial relations team (January 29).

NCB announces that since March 1984 620 men have been sacked from the mines and only 38 reinstated.

February 1985: Second Yorkshire Area Women Against Pit Closures conference held at Northern College (February 2).

Joint appeal by NUM and NACODS executives to NCB to reopen negotiations (February 8).

Brenda Greenwood wins case when she is charged with causing an obstruction and threatening behaviour likely to cause a breach of the peace (February 19).

Miners' Rally held in London. Speakers include Tony Benn, Denis Skinner and Ken Livingstone (February 24).

NCB claims 1464 new faces back at work (February 26).

Appeal for striking miners and their families published in the national press (February 27).

March 3 1985: NUM ends the strike. Special delegate conference in London votes 98–91 to return to work on March 5 without a settlement.

March 5 1985: Women and children join the miners' marches back to the pits, behind bands and banners.

Kent miners stay out on strike and continue to picket other coal fields to demand amnesty for sacked miners.

March 9 1985: International Women's Day rally at Chesterfield is attended by 25 000 women.

With acknowledgments to research by Barnsley Women Against Pit Closures: *People's History of Yorkshire* No. 12, Barnsley Women Against Pit Closures, Arc and Throstle Press, Todmorden.

Introduction

Since the end of the miners' strike in March 1985, the number of miners has been drastically reduced: from 172,363 to 114,974 in February 1987. This is mainly a result of the contraction of the industry planned by the government and the National Coal Board before the strike.

The contraction is itself part of a wider scenario within the European Community, where coalmining has been run down deliberately in favour of cheap imports of coal from countries outside the Community, mainly South Africa and Poland. Europe has chosen nuclear power because it is believed that the nuclear industry is the only energy producer which can guarantee consistent and unlimited supplies of power at stable prices.

An outsider might wonder why Britain had ever needed to enter into expensive investment in nuclear power stations, with so much energy already at its disposal. The answer lay in the Tory obsession with monetarist policies, which meant they could not tolerate any business which was not making a profit, even if it was contributing to the national wealth as a whole. The Tories also feared the strength of the miners' union, the National Union of Mineworkers, which had already brought one Tory government down in the 1970s. Margaret Thatcher's government decided that it had no security – and indeed, that there could be no prosperity for the country as a whole – unless the power of the unions was broken, particularly that of the miners' union.

1

Stocks of coal had to be high enough to ensure the continuance of power stupplies. Then the strike could be engineered by ensuring a proliferation of small-scale disputes over closures and redundancies throughout the coalfields.

The popular myth that it was Arthur Scargill who foolishly led the miners in a doomed 'Charge of the Light Brigade' thus makes nonsense. In fact Scargill was being pushed into a fight from the grassroots, where disputes had been breaking out at one pit and another a year before the major strike started. It was the members of the union who were beginning to rebel against their leaders. Tired of living on minimum social benefits, some engaged in individual pit disputes and then insisted that the rest of the uinion support them. If the NUM leaders had not agreed to national action when they did, they would have lost their jobs; and they knew it.

I was in Scotland throughout the strike, and it was at Polmaise, a small pit in Stirlingshire, that I first learned the reasons for the strike. Polmaise was told in January 1984 that it was to be closed, and the miners simply handed in their helmets and came out. Infuriated by lack of action from their national leaders – there had already been £15 million of new investment in this pit, stopped, they said, purely because of the animosity of the Coal Board's Scottish Area Director, Albert Wheeler – they invaded a meeting of the Scottish Executive of the NUM in Edinburgh to demand union support for their campaign to keep Polmaise open. The leaders were forced to allow the Polmaise men to tour the pits throughout Scotland, and support was readily forthcoming from many pits also under threat of closure.

'Everyone is running for cover, but there's no cover left,' said one Polmaise pit delegate. This was the reply over and over again when in the coming months miners were asked why they were striking: 'We've nowhere left to go. If the pit closes, there are no other jobs.'

For information about what was happening at the pits I went directly to the Polmaise delegate, John McCormack, a tidy, courteous, brisk Scot.

The case of the moves against Polmaise by the NCB was particularly curious. Down the deep shafts, there was at least 30 years' working of good coal lying behind geological faults which could be cut through with special cutting machinery. Polmaise had been a non-productive mine awaiting promised redevelopment for 15 months. At the time of the proposed closure, the Scottish NCB had already invested £15 million, as part of a £24 million deal, to open up the new seam.

The decision to stop investment in the pit had come after men at the Polmaise pit had refused to work with a group of miners transferred from Cardowan pit, closed after a long campaign by its workforce, many miles away near Glasgow. Polmaise said the NCB had broken its promise that miners already transferred out of the pit unwillingly to other pits further away would be the first to be allowed back down when the chance came.

Work on the new seam was suspended. Although they had been told six months earlier that there was 30 years new work for all of them in the pit, the decision was taken in January 1984 – after a winter when men simply sat down the pit, in enforced idleness, not allowed to work – to re-assess the pit and then to close it.

It was the apparent injustice of this that started the strike.

The striking miners were concerned about their families' plight. Early in the national strike they were cooking and serving meals to their families in the miners' welfare.

One of the wives confided to me: 'They are very good to us. They won't even let us do the washing up after they have cooked and served the meals. They call it a soup kitchen, but we always have a main course and sometimes soup as well, and for a treat, ice cream at the end. The real treat, of course, is a cup of tea.' Even in those early days, the plentiful tea which had kept the domestic wheels turning was already only a memory.

I did not see how they could bear the austerity of it all, remembering the dreariness of the war years, but they went on bearing it – and worse – for nearly another year. 'They would eat grass rather than give in now,' said another wife. 'The coal down in that mine shines like diamonds. It's wonderful. Yet the

Coal Board wants to shut the pit and drown it in water. We are not going to let them. We shall never give in.'

The village of Fallin, near the Polmaise pit, was then organised on collective lines. A miners' committee issued vouchers to families with which they bought meat at the butchers. (The shops joined in the voucher system.) The money came from other workers – at the Grangemouth docks, for example, some workers were giving 25 per cent of their wages every week to Fallin. The Imperial Tobacco factory workers who were also local, gave regularly and heavily to keep the families fed. The harder the times, the greater the solidarity.

At Polmaise, in August 1984, as in the coalfields throughout Britain, the women's support groups had reached a critical phase. The support could have weakened at that time, but in fact it was strengthened by a mass meeting and march in London of 15,000 women on 11 August which brought new strength to the strike and by the enormous efforts of the women's leaders to get the campaign to switch into a new gear, ready for the long haul through the winter months, with only a barren Christmas to look forward to. They were, of course, successful. When the strike ended in March, it was against the wishes of the women, who protested that they had not come so far, nor endured such hardship, only to be defeated at that point.

The Polmaise women had started collecting their own funds for the food and had taken over work at the miners' welfare food kitchen. The hire purchase, the pension subscriptions, the new carpets, the rent and, in some cases, the mortgage – all these preoccupations had been put aside until after the strike. They did not bother about clothes any more – how could they?

They were out with the collecting boxes in the streets of Glasgow, and soon, like miners' wives and relatives all over the country, they were standing up on platforms to make speeches to raise funds and flying abroad on fund-raising campaigns.

At Christmas, I was invited to the Polmaise children's Christmas party. There seemed to be police cars everywhere in those days, and even to drive into the yard of the miners' welfare made you feel as though you might be picked up and arrested. Inside with the bright lights there was a feeling of solid warmth, security and support and good humour such as I had rarely experienced before. If this was the subversion being fought by Mrs Thatcher and Mr Ian MacGregor, then it wore a strange face. These were, presumably, MacGregor's 'enemies within'. These 'enemies' were decent people, caring not only about their families' but about their neighbours' hardship, foregoing the chance of redundancy payments of up to £30,000 for the sake of keeping the jobs going. 'No one here would take it,' John McCormack told me.

'The miners' fathers and grandfathers worked in the mine. Everyone here knows everyone else and would soon find out about it.'

I kept close to Polmaise – the Scottish NUM headquarters was not responsive to journalists and its leaders were preaching a powerful anti-media message which later proved catastrophic to the miners, who needed all the friends they could get. But at pit level – at Cardowan, Monktonhall, Polkemmet, Bilston Glen – I found only friendliness and a desperate need to get across to any journalist who would listen the deep-seated sense of injustice. The villages had been turned into armed camps, and there had been arrests by police of innocent people outside their own homes – who was to tell of this if journalists did not do so?

Six months after the strike had ended, I wrote my last story about Polmaise. Though John McCormack had quickly been selected for redundancy by the Coal Board, in spite of his protests both to the NCB and his union, the pit, at least, had been reprieved. While other pits closed, the colliery, which had been in the vanguard of the national strike, was guaranteed £18 million, to be invested in it over a period of six years as a ten-mile tunnel was constructed to link it to a new complex of pits feeding a major power station at Longannet. One hundred workers had to be transferred or made redundant. Even so, if Polmaise remained open, the miners' wives who had been fighting for it knew there was still a chance that some time in the future that 'coal shining like diamonds' in the uncut face might be claimed at last. And the geological faults which had caused so many hold-ups before the strike were, said the miners, cut through easily and quickly without the necessity for all the costly machinery which the engineers had said they would need.

Now selected pits throughout Britain are being modernised and are showing a profit. Miners are willingly taking redundancy and the nuclear industry is forging ahead. Both the management and workforce in the pits, some of which are currently breaking productivity records, are operating so well after the departure of Sir Ian MacGregor that it raises the suspicion that good management could have brought about the same results without a strike at all and the intense suffering that that engendered.

It was easy and convenient to discuss the strike in personal terms of a political battle between Arthur Scargill and Margaret Thatcher, with Ian MacGregor, Chairman of the National Coal Board, at her right hand. In fact, however, it had far more to do with the facts of life in the pit villages, and this was what concerned the miners' wives. This book is about their lives during the strike and what the strike meant for them.

The fight for jobs was at the core of the women's support, without which the strike could never have kept going for more than a few months. By 1984, women knew what the face of unemployment looked like. The picture was depression and despair, which destroyed the life of a family. It was drink, degradation, homelessness and drugs for the young, the slow destruction of self-sufficient communities, illness, suicide and the drawn-out extinction of hope. This seemed to be the future for those who had been Britain's proudest and strongest skilled workers, whose skills below ground had always been interdependent, who had learned about communities from the necessity of working together and trusting each other down the pit. They loved their villages. They hated being bussed to faraway pits to take the jobs of older men who had been unwillingly forced into redundancy.

The miners' strike was the opportunity for women in

coalmining communities to make their voice heard on a matter of major policy, and they seized it. The consequences were far-reaching and have not yet been fully realised. The vehemence of their support for coal suprised even the miners. Their work kept the strike going and would have prolonged it past the date when the leaders decided to call a halt. And, as the strike went on and the women were able to draw on the support of other political groups, they began increasingly to connect their struggle with the political battle that was already under way against all forms of nuclear power.

The 'politicisation' of the women was much referred to by journalists during the strike. Yet, with the exception of Scotland, where the NUM recognised the women's contribution to the strike by allowing them to become associate members of the NUM, women were barred from the miners' union. Their request for associate membership was turned down at the first national conference after the strike.

It was a different matter so far as international politics were concerned. Women were awakened to the potential power of the people in grassroots politics. They joined forces with nuclear disarmers in Britain, and after the strike formed an organisation with them called 'Links'. They met regularly and joined cause with black miners in Namibia working in appalling conditions to provide uranium for British Nuclear Fuels Limited, and with the dispossessed Pacific islanders whose homes were used for the testing of nuclear weapons later deployed in Britain at Greenham and Faslane.

The fact that there is enough food to feed the entire population of the world, and yet millions starve because of the way international finance is organised, became the concern of Women Against Pit Closures, the main organisation of the miners' wives, which continued after the strike.

The explosion at Chernobyl in Russia which spread dangerously high levels of radioactivity over the whole of Europe demonstrated the high risk involved in nuclear energy. Could coal, although to some extent polluting, possibly be as dangerous as a source of power which not only induces cancer but, in cases of accident or error, can render a whole land uninhabitable and condemn thousands to a slow and painful death?

The leap into nuclear power was not started by the Tory government. They simply accelerated its development. However, the political allegiance to nuclear power has faltered perceptibly in the wake of Chernobyl. Quite apart from the immediate effects of the disaster on farming land and cattle, and the anxieties it has caused over irradiated milk and food, there is conclusive and damning evidence in recently published reports of abnormally high rates of leukaemia to be found in children who live near nuclear plants.

Women Against Pit Closures has found itself part of the vanguard of a new movement against nuclear energy. The miners may oppose nuclear power because they want to keep their jobs down the pits, but the women oppose it because they also fear the effects of nuclear accidents on future generations and the rising levels of radioactivity.

Sadly, little progress has yet been made with what is actually the most important of women's objectives: a truly equal share in the way the country is run. Until women cease to be exploited in every country in the world – and this includes those countries that claim to be revolutionary – and take their full rightful share in influence and decision-making at every level, no responsible government can exist anywhere. In West Germany, the Greens Party introduced a 50 per cent share of power for women at its inception, and has surprised Europe by the rapidity of the growth of support for its extremely radical proposals. Its success is, as I see it, actually *because of* its radical constitution.

During the miners' strike, the strength to be gained through the use of the whole of women's potential was clearly demonstrated. Will that potential be once more neglected now that particular crisis has passed? Or will the women succeed in sustaining their solidarity, and be able to broaden their objectives to affect a wider world?

There are some signs that this happening, though much is

loaded against the women. It took 40 years from the time when all men were given the vote in Britain for the working-class party to gain power in parliament. It is 60 years since women gained the vote, but their democratic representation is still negligible. The actions of the women in the miners' strike formed a small but important part of the move towards righting this imbalance. Their place in the history of feminism, as well as in mining history, is assured.

A note on naming

Throughout the book I have tried to use the phrase 'women in the mining communities' to describe the subjects of this story. However this is a long and clumsy phrase, and too often I have had to resort to the less precise 'miners' wives' for the sake of readability. Apologies to the mothers and the daughters; and to the wives, who of course are women before they are wives.

1.

Headlong into Politics

The 1984 strike was about jobs, whereas the strikes of 1972 and 1974 had been about pay. The miners' wives' response in 1984 was spontaneous, and quickly grew in strength to such a degree that the miners would have found it hard to give up their strike even if they had wanted to.

A national ballot might have kept public opinion happier, but it would have made no difference to the strike. Polmaise and Cortonwood and Maerdy pit in the Rhondda would have stayed on strike, even if no other pit in the country had supported them. No one thought that going down the pit was a great life for a young man. It was not even well paid any more in many of the older pits. Many surface workers made only £80 per week, but it was a job. As John McCormack, the Polmaise pit delegate, said: 'We have nothing to lose any more. If our pit closes, there is nowhere else for us to go.'

The determination of the women was linked to that of the young miners. They did not want to see their husbands on the dole. Even more, they could not tolerate the thought of their children, for whom they had had so many secret dreams, constantly being rejected by employers, and having to face unemployment. There was nowhere for these young men to emigrate to any more. The US, Canada, Australia and Europe were now blocked by their own unemployment problems. Young people who left to seek jobs in London, they knew, often ended up living as criminals, or homeless and on heroin. And the numbers of unemployed sleeping rough in London and other cities had reached epidemic proportions.

The young, single miners, under the new Department of Health and Social Security laws, received no money to live on because they were deemed to get £16 a week from the NUM – whereas in fact the NUM did not pay strike money. They received a few pounds for picketing expenses – and that was all. Their lot was the hardest, and they were difficult to help because of their pride.

For women outside the pit villages it was difficult to grasp the miners' wives' fierce allegiance to the local pit and its coal. Previously, even if a bright child with a number of O and A levels could not get a job outside there had always been the job in the pit to turn to. Now this was no longer the case; increasingly the mines were disappearing.

Women in the pit towns and villages had always known about the mining of coal. They knew where faces were being opened up, what the political reasons were for closing others, where seams were rich and where others were played out. They lived with coal mining, as their mothers had done. They knew more about it than many at NCB headquarters in London.

So when they pleaded the case against pit closures, they were sure of their ground.

A Barnsley rally, to which 10,000 women turned up from all over the country early in the strike, had shown the spontaneity of the movement. 'The work of the women in the strike has provided inspiration to the women's movement here in Britain, and internationally. There can be no turning back. Too many women have been arrested. Women are in the vanguard of the strike. They have changed. They are getting an education in politics.'

At Hatfield Main, one of Yorkshire's largest collieries, which had employed 1,300 men and was now under threat of closure, Lynn Clegg, a young wife of a miner with twin boys, told how she became involved with support for the struggle against pit closures. This involvement was long before the strike:

When I saw on television about two years ago they were going to close Lewis Merthyr pit in Wales I couldn't get over it. I felt so sad. I felt I had to do something . . . So I started to organise a campaign against closure at Hatfield. I didn't have any lead about what to do. I just went round different people's houses with Carol, my neighbour, and asked them their feelings. We decided to lobby the main NUM branch meeting about taking strike action to support Lewis Merthyr. We worked hard and made a banner and got a dozen or so women to support us. Many were saying Lewis Merthyr is only one pit, they won't close Hatfield Main. But I could see what was going to happen. The ballot went against strike action then, and the women all disappeared. But when the strike started in 1984 we got together again. We were organised from the first week of the strike. We knew what to do, straight away. We had a meeting in the Broadway Hotel, our local pub, and that was how it got started.

Coming Together

There was no doubt the women's pride in their communities was justified. In the pit villages there was comparatively little crime. The old mixed with the young at the miners' welfare halls. In a place where everyone knew each other you could walk in safety, leave property unlocked – even your own front door – and no one would bother you. There is nowhere in the world that can give a greater feeling of security and protection to a visitor than a friendly pit village. Even so, as the strike wore on, it was this very security which was to be threatened by the confrontation between police and pickets.

Nevertheless, both the miners and the women were refusing to be dwarfed. Because of the isolation of the pit communities and in spite of the transfers, they had not realised quite how bad things had become in the world outside. The Welsh were right when they claimed that there would have been more active support from other trade unionists if they had gone on strike in

1982. Now the atmosphere in the country had become so poisoned by fear, insecurity and by unemployment, which was treated as if it were a disease rather than as a planned consequence of government policy, that support for the miners was from the beginning more covert than active.

The miners' wives couldn't understand the lack of support from other trade unionists. Their case for the protection of jobs, even if it meant subsidising pits, seemed such a just cause, so vital to the nation, that they could not comprehend why everyone did not immediately follow them. They were, in fact, out of touch, as they realised in the end. The fear of losing a job, or the degradation of having to queue at a specific centre for the dole and social security money without being able to move round the country freely, had taken away any appetite for risk-taking. All over Britain, families were battening down the hatches. Nowadays, you looked after your own and did not ask too many questions. If you were fairly rich and middle-class, you did not consider your children to be unemployed; they were travelling or studying, or running some original little business which did not quite manage to make a profit. If you were working-class, your children were well and truly unemployed or else hanging desperately on to a job. Whatever the situation was, it took most of the family energies to sustain the position, and increasingly people were falling apart under the strain.

With the lack of support from the outside world, mining families were coming together more strongly than ever before. (Eventually, in fact, young unemployed from the cities found a new strength and interest by joining the miners' picket lines all over the country.)

Education

There are miners' wives who freely admit they never bothered to vote before the strike. And if anyone is shocked by this, first consider their position. All political parties are run by men. Every political platform throughout the world is dominated by men, East and West, Communist and capitalist. The pits were run by men and the income came from men. Often, the miners' wives did not even have the freedom to go out to work, because they were tied to the ritual of being around to provide a meal at the end of a shift. Mining, whether on the surface or the face, is physically exhausting, and pit villages do not have handy eating places like works canteens.

So what was the point of voting for yet another lot of men? What possible difference could it make to womens' lives? No one ever put forward a proper manifesto for them; a programme that could make their lives better, or provide them with more personal money, or give them a greater say in the way things were run.

Certainly, many women did not take trade unions seriously. What did the unions really care about in the women's lives?

It is said by women in the support groups that when they started there were women who did not know what the initials TUC stood for. If they were to win the respect of the miners' union delegates, however, union jargon had to trip off their tongues as if they were thoroughly used to it.

Jean Miller, a founder of Barnsley Women Against Pit Closures, tells how one of the first exercises of the women in this group was to educate themselves in union politics and the politics of the world outside. Jean, politicised early in life through membership of the Young Communist League, had travelled to trade union congresses and peace meetings in Europe and had been at Greenham Common. She welcomed the chance to share her political knowledge. In the Barnsley area there were many women who were thirsty for information once they realised how politics were affecting their lives through pit closures.

A women's conference at the Northern College in Yorkshire in the summer of 1984 was crucial for helping women to get this groundwork done. Women needed to be together for self-education. Such conferences, and courses set up after they had taken place, were necessary because one or two male trade unionists taking the mickey could make women – and men, too, for that matter – scared to ask basic questions for fear of looking stupid.

Watching television was another way for women to educate themselves. In spite of the criticisms of bias against television political coverage, the bulletins in fact sharpened the appetite for politics in the pit communities.

Pauline Radford, from the Blidworth Women's Support Group near Mansfield, in Nottinghamshire, explained: 'Before the strike, we'd sit and watch a television party political broadcast and think "Oh no! I'm not watching this boring stuff", and switch it off. But now you watch a party political broadcast whatever party it is, and you sit glued to it.'

'You shout at them, don't you?' said Susan Petney, also from Blidworth.

'Yes, specially the SDP. The Tories, well . . . though even the backbench Tories can see Thatcher's going too far with everything.'

Public Speaking

Women, who had never before been outside their own villages and had never even spoken on a platform at a Miners' Welfare meeting, started to make speeches all over the country – even though they shook with fright to start with. They flew to Europe and further afield to raise funds. Broadcasting became an everyday event for these normally housebound women.

Women had to learn the technique of public speaking. This they did by applying the simple principle of jumping in at the deep end. One week the wife of a Polmaise miner was organising a jumble sale to raise funds, adopting the traditional woman's role. A few months later she was flying to London to present the miners' case for keeping pits open on TV AM, and no one in the village of Fallin thought it even mildly unusual. The women were now all over the place, forgetting their nerves in order to get money for a cause they believed in so passionately.

The Rhondda women found themselves speaking on the same platform as, for example, Neil Kinnock and Tony Benn. Through this they discovered they were a greater draw to an audience than politicians. All they had to do was to say clearly what they really felt and hoped for, to set out sensible and logical proposals for how society should be run and why government plans for pit closures were wrong – and they got an immediate response. People were looking for a message, and the miners' wives seemed to have one.

Doreen Humber, from the Blidworth group, described her experience of public speaking at Cambridge, eight months after the strike started.

There were about 600 people and Pauline [Radford], spoke and then I spoke. My husband was there and it was the first time since it's started that he'd heard me give a political speech. Pauline spoke about what we do in the village hall and feeding the kids and I spoke about the strike. I was really going on and getting carried away. They kept pushing notes in front of me which said 'shut up now', 'shut up now', but I didn't even see the notes; I was just carried away. When I finished and came off the stage, my husband came up to me and gave me a kiss. He said, 'That speech was fantastic'. It amazed him that I could stand up there and speak politics. So all those things that I've gone out and learned; it took a meeting for him to attend to listen to me speaking to realise how I'd come forward in eight months.

Pauline Radford said that before the strike she had never thought of

just getting up one morning and going off to London for a few days, because I'd never have dreamed of leaving the kids and because I didn't believe my husband was capable of looking after them the same as I was. And yet I've found that he is as capable as I am and that I can leave them for a few days and come back. They think more of you when you come back.

The kids seem to think it's great that mum goes off to meetings and things like that, so it doesn't do them any harm. Things don't just wrap up because mum's not around. Dad can take over.

Support Groups

Support groups, comprising miners' wives and other women closely associated with mining communities were very quickly formed, once the strike had started, up and down the country, to help the striking miners.

In Wales, 106 women's support groups were organised from Cardiff, covering 27 pits right across South Wales.

The Welsh support co-ordinating group started after the conference at Northern College in Yorkshire.

Seven Welsh women attended the conference and immediately afterwards started to organise the South Wales support groups and held their first meeting. 'You be chairman, Kath,' they said to Kath Jones. It was in that simple way that it started.

The South Wales organiser, Kath Jones, had just retired from British Telecom where she had been a trade union official, only to find that she was now working harder than ever in her life before.

Kath had married into a mining family and had lived in Wales for 30 years. She remembered her father-in-law's tales of the work camps for the unemployed miners in the 1930s when they lived behind wire fences and were paid a few pence a week. Originally she had come from the Isle of Dogs in the East End of London and had been much affected by the deliberate destruction by the planners of the East End communities. The planners may have had good intentions, but little knowledge of what human beings were about. But in one stroke they had shattered the neighbourliness, the warmth of support and the extended family network that had acted as a barrier against poverty and crime. People in the East End were either forced into the isolation of tower blocks, or were forced out to New Towns or satellite suburbs in other cities, as remote from their relatives and friends as if they had emigrated. The areas of east and south London, famous throughout the world for their character and comradeship, had been effectively destroyed, and people like Kath Jones had not forgotten this. Small, neat and essentially moderate, her whole life was now turned to helping the organisation of the miners' support groups.

It was not an easy job for the women. There were families to reach in seven of the deep Welsh valleys. Getting up and down these was difficult – and so was finding the way. Swansea itself was isolated, and had no soup kitchens.

Because of the pit transfer system some families lived as far as 50 miles from the pits. The organising group became intensely politically interesting to a number of groups in Cardiff – trade unionists, left-wing groups and radical causes. Eventually a deep split emerged. In the Welsh Women Against Pit Closures, a takeover by Socialist Action was suspected. The Women's Support Groups withdrew and started to run their own programme of food and fund raising. Kath Jones found the militant left worrying and was a leader of the move to separate the support groups from the Welsh Women Against Pit Closures branches penetrated by Socialist Action.

The Barnsley March

The Yorkshire women in Barnsley were among the first to organise support groups for the miners. A group of neighbours inserted a paragraph in a local paper advertising a meeting to decide how they could best help the strikers. To their amazement, a small front room was crowded with would-be supporters. This was how the Barnsley Women Against Pit Closures was formed.

At the weekly meeting of Barnsley Women Against Pit Closures on 22 April 1984, the women decided to hold a national, all-women rally, with a march through Barnsley. They thought this would be the best way of uniting the women nationally who were already forming themselves into support groups.

It was fixed for 12 May, only 20 days after the initial meeting.

The women had not realised that a rally would need so much organising. Key areas were informed – Durham, Nottingham, Wales, Staffordshire, Scotland, Leicestershire, Lancashire and Yorkshire – about the rally and people were asked to pass on the message. They had allowed a very short time to get it together – they were only guessing when they told the police that 2,000 would turn up, but then they found that Barnsley Civic Hall was not big enough to hold that number. The manager arranged a public address system for an overflow meeting.

On the day, wrote one of the organisers: 'The coaches arrived – one, two, three, they kept coming – thirty and then forty, thousands and thousands of women from all over the country.' It was far more than the police or anyone had expected.

They had two male speakers – Arthur Scargill and Jack Taylor, the Yorkshire NUM President – and three women speakers – Lorraine Bowler of Barnsley, Annette Holroyd of Nottingham and Maureen Douglass of Doncaster.

Arthur Scargill and Jack Taylor suggested the women should lead the march, with themselves a couple of rows behind, surrounded by children. The other men marched at the back.

Jean Miller describes the day.

It sounded impossible, though no one had any doubts we could do it. But nobody dreamt it would be so huge. They came from everywhere. We had told the police to expect quite small numbers, but they were having to send the coaches outside the town to park; there was no more room in Barnsley.

There were at least 10,000. That was the press estimate and I think there were more. Barnsley is quite a small town and we started to worry that the front of the march would meet the back!

We had all the women in the front, with Arthur Scargill at the head but the rest of the men at the back. The women were so excited about being at the front – for some of them, it was the first rally they had ever been to.

The rally was held in the Civic Hall, and we only let women in.

Jean was a Greenham woman who had been to many political and peace rallies.

This was truly the most electrifying experience of my life. The atmosphere was tremendous. There were so many women in there it felt as though the floor was going to collapse. They were waving banners and cheering. There were just short speeches.

I can remember every detail of that day. I could never forget it.

The Civic Hall meeting was only for women, and men were asked to stay out, the only exceptions being the two male speakers on the platform. The women, singing, chanting and shouting, filled the hall. Different accents and different banners were heard and seen, from Wales, Kent, Durham, Barnsley, Sheffield, Staffordshire, with women weeping with emotion. 'As I stood there looking at them,' wrote one woman, 'I thought we can't and won't lose anything, let alone this strike, with women like these fighting together.'

It was the Barnsley march that started things off. It was after this that the women started contacting groups from outside their own areas, making plans, organising and getting together on a national basis. That year, Jean, like other women, went to Belgium, Holland and France on fund-raising trips and to speak on foreign platforms to trade unionists about the strike. It was the Barnsley march, too, which helped contribute towards the formation of the national Women Against Pit Closures.

It was a turning point, not only in the strike, but in the working-class feminist movement as a whole.

The National Women's Organisation

It was at Chesterfield that a national conference of women's action groups, held on 10 and 11 November 1984, founded the new National Women's Organisation.

Betty Heathfield, a founder member, put a high priority on this organisation. It would mean that the solidarity and mutual support the women had established during the strike would not be lost if they could keep the organisation going after the strike had ended. A list of aims was drawn up which read:

1. To consolidate the National Women's Organisation and ensure victory for the National Union of Mineworkers in their present struggle; to prevent pit closures and protect mining communities for the future.
2. To further strengthen the organisation of women's groups which has been built up during the 1984 miners' strike.
3. To develop a relationship between the National Union of Mineworkers and the Women's Organisation at all levels.
4. To campaign on issues which affect mining communities, particularly peace, jobs, health and education.
5. To promote and develop education for working-class women.
6. To publicise the activities of the National Women's Organisation at all levels.

It had its splits and disagreements but finally was incorporated into the Women Against Pit Closures national organisation, which is now flourishing and growing.

Women Against Pit Closures

Women Against Pit Closures was formed shortly before the big march and rally against pit closures by women from coalfields all over Britain in London in August 1984.

The founding of Women Against Pit Closures in Barnsley

came about through a letter to the Barnsley *Chronicle*, expressing the support of a group of women for the striking miners, with an invitation to like-minded women to join them. The response was immediate. From the small meeting in a front room shortly after the strike started sprang the national linking of women's groups into this one organisation.

Its aims include the promotion and development of education for working-class women and campaigns on all issues which affect mining communities, particularly peace, jobs, health and education, and the issues of nuclear power and nuclear weapons. Also the organisation aims to develop a relationship between the NUM and women's organisations at all levels.

It remains an organisation for miners' families, but has 25 per cent ex officio members consisting of women who have given an unusual amount of support in a number of ways to Women Against Pit Closures, both during and after the strike. The percentage of 75 per cent miners' families and 25 per cent members outside the communities was agreed after a number of meetings and conferences.

International Politics

The women were absorbing every bit of information about pits and national and international politics they could get hold of, and starting to apply their knowledge. What was happening in Soweto, in Chile, or at Greenham Common became relevant to them, they said, because they saw very strong links with their own situations. Women all over the world were trying to preserve similar values, trying to defend their families from external barbarism committed by – usually male – politicians. There was even more. The women could see that what was happening in the destruction of their pit villages was a microcosm of what was happening in the world at large, where men had almost all the power. The men possessed too little wisdom and were behaving delinquently. Women had hardly any power at all, and there was a very uneven spread of world resources. It sickened the miners' wives to think of the waste and greed of the West and the poverty of the East. The women of the Third World became their concern, too.

Linda King, of Ollerton Colliery Women's Support Group, had not thought much about international politics until she went to Colchester, which gave support to Ollerton during the strike. 'I've met a great bunch of people I'd never have met if it hadn't been for the strike – including the legal advisers. We've had support from teachers and social workers a long way away from where we are. It's been fantastic.'

The Ollerton Colliery Women's Support Group also had support from the Chileans. In Norwich, she and the other women met a group of Chilean exiles. They found they had a lot in common.

The Chilean people have been great to us. You see, they know what it's like to go through this, better than we know ourselves. They are lovely people. After the strike, there is no way we are going to lose touch with them, and the people in Norwich who helped us. All the things they've done for us – they took the kids down for a week's holiday. They'd come up on a Sunday in the school holidays and take the kids back with them. We are going to keep on going down there and they will come up for our monthly meeting. Whatever happens, we can't let the contacts go. There are people we have got to know, things we have learned that would never have happened if it hadn't been for the strike. None of us are the same as we were before. Once the strike is over, there's decorating to do and things to put right in the home that got left for so long, but we still want to keep in touch with all the people we met, especially the women.

The women, some for the first time, started to learn about the monetarist political system in Chile and at what cost in terms of imprisonment and torture it had been imposed, and about Nicaragua, nuclear weapons, miners in America and West Indians in Brixton. They studied television documentaries and news programmes, as well as learning from people they were now meeting on their fund-raising tours.

It was quite common for the women in the support groups to go to France, West Germany, Holland, Italy or Scandinavia, as guests of the trade unions or of environment groups. They also went to countries further away such as Finland or Iceland and made a number of trips to countries in Eastern Europe.

After the visit by the NUM chief executive, Roger Windsor, to Colonel Gadafy in Libya, of which much political mileage was made about Libyan support for the miners' strike, Susan Petney of Blidworth said:

> It was blown up out of proportion. When we saw it on television we were shouting back at the set, 'What about all the oil we get from Libya?' and, 'Do you know that this country is exporting leg irons to South Africa?' Before the strike, if we hadn't known about these things, then we'd have said, 'Well, yes, they are right there, we shouldn't have gone to see Colonel Gadafy.' But we suddenly realised there were two sides to everything. Now we question everything!

Once people start to question, there is no end to it. The women who started to question the political system during the strike will continue to do so. They will also start to question the way the NUM is run, and the way women's lives are predetermined, not only by their sex, but often by men for their own convenience. There are many miners who will accept this questioning and even welcome it. There are many others, however, who are finding it is making their lives more difficult.

Women and the Labour Party

Many issues remain for the miners' wives, according to Kay Sutcliffe, Chairwoman of Kent Women's Support groups.

The miners' wives have given the women's movement an

extra voice. We'd like to see them moving into political life, not just fighting for their own communities. What we need to do is work together and get women organised into the Labour Party and fighting in their own areas, get on local councils and put forward as candidates to strengthen the labour movement. The labour movement is very weak at present and the leadership leaves a lot to be desired. But there is a strong rank and file which needs co-ordinating. The Labour Party and the TUC should look at how they have failed over the past 12 months of the strike and start to think what they can do for the working class – which is what they were elected for.

A year after the strike ended in March 1985, the fight for women's representation in the Labour Party had scarcely even begun. There were no more than a sprinkling of women Parliamentary candidates through the country and women had no effective voice on the Labour Party National Executive. The Labour Party was going into the next election with the same old male middle-class image.

Whether the Labour Party can use the new strength and determination of the women to build up its own strength remains to be seen. Clearly, there are still divisions within the party and within the union movements which seem likely to continue. But until the result of the next election in the mid-1980s is known, it will not be obvious how influential the 'green' movement has been in breaking up the established order in the Labour Party, the working-class organisations and the trade unions. The miners' support groups and the miners themselves, determinedly anti-nuclear and internationalist in outlook, are now ranked among the 'greens'.

Exploitation of the Women

There is no doubt that miners' wives have been, and are still, exploited by their husbands. The lives the women lead are bound up with, and controlled by, the men's jobs.

In his book, *The Militancy of British Miners*, Professor Vic Allen, an authority on industrial relations and conditions in the mining industry, claims that mining families, centred around women, have functioned as vital elements in the organisation of mining.

In what might appear to be an incredibly uncanny fashion, every detail of the immediate environment of the miners – their leisure, their homes, family relationships, wives and children – has served the structure of their existence, namely the provision of labour power with given skills in required quantities at the right times. Nothing and no one has been spared . . . It has not been a machiavellian operation; there have been no villains. It has been simply a case of the basic structural needs of the situation dominating everything else, moulding everything to suit its own peculiar requirements. In this process women and wives have been adapted to meet the needs of mining as effectively as miners themselves.

Professor Allen points out that women made sure, through a variety of activities, that the coal-owners would have an adequate supply of male workers tramping to the pits each day and night, and that this was done at no cost to the employers, for the domestic labour had no price on it. It suited employers that, while men derived power and status from their involvement in market-determined production, the family household activities were devalued, without price or status. 'It was not even designated as work. Women received only their subsistence, paid in kind, in return for their labour.' For some, there was also full- or part-time labour in the cotton or textile industries, when the capitalist system required it.

So long as domestic labour was not treated as a marketable commodity and home-working was dismissed as a peripheral phenomenon then family services could be regarded as free goods for employers and female labour could be degraded in whatever form it was used.

The manner in which a division of labour was wrought between miners and womenfolk was as effective as any that had been created in the production process and was as necessary for that process. It was supported and justified by ideas about women and their relationships with men which had a basis in women's experience. Women concerned about households wanted regular wages so they preferred miners to be consistent and responsible workers, abstemious workers, hard workers.

Professor Allen discusses the encouragement and legitimisation of ideas about 'man's work' and responsibility of the women in the home, the virtue of obedience to a man's wishes, of subordination to his needs. These ideas, communicated through education, religion and the media, as well as literature, 'consolidated the divisions between men and women by becoming part of their consciousness, expressed in the conviction that the division was right, indeed natural.'

The majority of miners come from mining families, in spite of the incidence of disease and injury in the job, he points out. The mining family, therefore, serves to perpetuate the mining industry. Anything which destroys mining families is creating problems for the future of the industry.

In 1987, when the pits as well as the people who work in them are being scrapped in favour of nuclear power, the women are also becoming less necessary to the industry, although they have always shown a loyalty to their husbands' work, to the local mines and to the very seams of coal within them.

The miners' wives are in a unique quandary. They are a necessary part of a skilled manual job in which they can never participate and in most cases do not even want to. Outside mining, women can be teachers, executives and even Church ministers. They have a choice. The miner's wife has no choice. That is why, during the strike, mining women in the support groups were so insistent that the strike was producing a totally new women's movement, that it was the first to have its roots in the working class.

They wanted to keep their solidarity. They wanted to remain sisters and not compete with each other like successful middle-class career women in a rat race copied from middle-class male society. In fact, they wanted to do no less than dig up the roots of society, shake them, clean them, and plant them again in a better soil.

In their bones they had always known they were exploited but they knew that at least their exploitation paralleled that of the men they shared their lives with. That is why miners' wives don't, on the whole, take their resentment of the past out on the miners of the present. They complain about their husbands' prejudices but they are setting out to change them – in between looking after the kids and getting the meals ready for the end of the shift. If the miners grasp even half of what these remarkable women are about, they will set about helping them to fight for the new society they long for.

A Working-Class Women's Movement

Betty Heathfield said 'In our companionship with our men, our common struggle, we've wiped out the myth of the working-class wife.'

What made up the myth of the working-class wife? That they had no interests outside their homes? That they did not make the political links between their own condition and what was happening in government? That they did not feel strong enough to change things through their own solidarity? That women were naturally right-wing and self-absorbed?

If this indeed were so, it was an unfair myth. Working-class women had simply not had the time to do things before. But, now that their husbands were on strike, men were taking over a share of the housekeeping, looking after the children and queuing up for food parcels at the soup kitchens. Now women had the time. In a few instances they started to behave according to the pattern of middle-class women that feminists despised – arranging coffee mornings and polite get-togethers, jumble sales and social gatherings. The majority, however, went for full-blooded change, modelling themselves on no one – and certainly not on men.

The women in 1984–85 were determined that it was going to be a truly working-class women's movement, and that no one from outside was going to patronise them, which they felt had happened with upper-class women in 1926.

Florence Anderson of the Eppleton Area Miners' Wives' Support Group in Durham, said after the strike:

All the women in our support group had connections with the mining community. That was a rule we made at the start. We really didn't want any outsiders in our kitchen, or professional do-gooders. We said it wasn't going to be like 1926, with people shuffling up to the soup kitchens demoralised and degraded. It was going to be miners' wives, miners' mothers, miners' sisters serving miners and their wives and families.

We didn't want any sort of intellectuals coming down to play around in soup kitchens. It was a working-class women's movement and that's why we were so proud of it. We kept it like that, because we said coming into the kitchen should be like coming home. Our kitchen was popular because we said everybody had to be made welcome. It was our own feeding our own. There was no feeling about it. We had no outsiders. In fact, we got no help from the Labour Party in Hetton at all. All we had from the Hetton Labour Party, in a mining community, was half the proceeds of a dance held in November, and we contributed to that because we all went along there and sat at the back and were never even mentioned. I think the Labour Party wasn't more involved because the miners' wives got together and took the lead from the start.

Kate Whiteside, the organiser of the Chesterfield support group, started organising during the by-election won by Tony Benn during the previous year. It was good practice. By

November 1983 they had the women's action group going, ready for the coming strike. Tony Benn, they said, had been very helpful to them. Kate said:

> This is totally unique. Most of the women have never done anything like this before. But they are frightened of being called feminists, or of ending up like middle-class women.
>
> Now they want to know more about *everything*, not just the mines. A lot of women are saying new doors have opened for them. We've already started talking about providing education for women's groups.

Kate regarded the women's support movement during the strike as 'the first truly working-class women's movement'. It was the first time in history that working-class women had been so organised. 'When the strike is over, and men go back to work, the whole family life is going to be totally different. Men and women are going to have to sit down and discuss this before it happens so they are prepared for it.'

In Scotland and Wales and Kent and Yorkshire, and everywhere where there were still pits and villages, women told me they had seen for the first time how it was possible radically to change not only their own lives but those of their children. Now they had a vision of changing the world, operating from a working-class base.

2.
Something Else in the House

When the women, encouraged by the miners, first started to form support groups they could scarcely have foreseen the consequences of their actions.

What began as organisations to feed the families and the young, single miners who received no social security money, ended as a new women's movement.

The young women, already less bound by the conventions of the mining villages than their mothers, were the first to branch out into picketing, passive resistance, and the handing over of a large part of child-care and house-cleaning to the miners. Older women were more involved with traditional women's work of fund raising, soup kitchens and food parcels. Adapting to the strike, however, really had very little to do with age. The support groups were impressive for their mixture of ages, and the way the women got on so well together. They achieved a new physical independence and self-reliance, as they were called on to deal with hardship, danger and deprivation without male help.

The miners, too, when they were not picketing or travelling to conferences or fund-raising, discovered their worlds were being turned upside down. They learned about solitude and the self-discipline and domestic skills needed for running a home, and they also, for the first time, learnt to enjoy their children.

In most cases, this reversal of the sexes' usual roles brought benefits. But many of the women had been starved of any independence and freedom to use their natural resourcefulness and brains. The sudden rush of independence and acquisition of new responsibilities were heady experiences and the women were reluctant to relinquish these when the strike came to an end. The result was tangled marriages and ill-concealed resentments which persist to this day. Many marriages have broken up as a result of the strike, although others have been strengthened.

Fund Raising

Lynn Clegg from Yorkshire was on the picket line and launched into fund-raising.

> We made a lot of contacts in London. I used to take the kids and stay with friends and they would look after them while I went fund-raising. I collected for the women's support and Tony [her husband] on behalf of the main NUM branch. We used to split up and go off to separate meetings. I went to a meeting at the *Sunday Times* EEPTU chapel and got £200. On the way home I got mugged in Brixton. They took it all – and my bracelet and £5 of my own. They were four black youths; they must have had a field day when they found how much they had got. But they must have known it was collected for the miners – the envelope was covered with miners' stickers. I blamed the system, the Tory government, the way the blacks are treated with no jobs; it's very sad.

In Scotland the women went fund-raising, with the first ones to do so being arrested in Glasgow. For a time, a teabag in the village of Fallin, opposite the Polmaise colliery, was a luxury. By the summer, however, the fund raising was becoming successful; the women had overcome their nerves and had become resourceful public speakers and broadcasters, and it was clear that, though life was hard, no one was going to starve.

Stirling council provided help. Workers at the Grangemouth docks agreed to a levy of 20 per cent of their wages. Although Scotswomen were a long way behind their sisters in England and Wales in some aspects of feminist awareness they nevertheless occupied historically a strong matriarchal position. They found themselves being propelled willy-nilly towards feminism by the demands of the strike. 'Their fight is only just beginning,' said one of the leaders of Stirling council which had supported them. 'When it is over, we have to see they get re-education. They have known no freedom. Now they have come this far, they must not go back.'

The Soup Kitchens

A pit village was the ideal environment for the start of the soup kitchens which were to save the miners from starving and from going back to work. It seemed almost incredible to those old enough to remember the dark tales of the 1930s that soup kitchens should have returned to the Welfare State. There was a nightmare quality about the situation.

In Yorkshire, Armthorpe, a community with a prosperous air (by August reduced to the state of impending civil war) was the first to start communal feeding and organising the transport of food to outlying areas.

The manager of the Broadway Hotel near Hatfield Main colliery used to be a small businessman until he was hit by recession. The miners were his clients. He also believed in their case. He put the whole of the big pub, with its spacious meeting rooms and kitchens, at the disposal of the women's support groups for the cooking and serving of meals. A reconversion of the pub had already started, and that was being carried out as well during the strike. Nothing stopped. A few weeks after the end of the strike, new velvet covers were on the banquettes, and the kitchens and bars were back to normal. 'But they were our greatest days. It was a wonderful feeling of comradeship, of helping each other. I shall never forget it,' he said.

'Hatfield Main had four kitchens serving about 1,800 meals a day, and the kitchens covered men from other pits who worked in other areas but lived here,' said Lynn Clegg.

The running of the soup kitchens in the Nottingham coalfields was very difficult, both because of the opposition to women getting premises and because of the crackdown by police on visiting Yorkshire pickets who often came to the soup kitchens.

In Scotland, the soup kitchens were strongly supported by local authorities such as Glasgow, Edinburgh and Stirling, which provided money, space, accommodation, and advice – and also froze rents.

At Polmaise the women quickly organised themselves, with the help of the NUM, into producing meals at the miners' welfare clubs. From the beginning, the men ran the meals, issued meal vouchers to families from a communal fund and did the washing up.

Joyce Coutts was secretary of the Lothian Women's Committee which co-ordinated the 28 support groups in the regions set up by the wives of the miners at Bilston Glen and Monktonhall, and she has two children. She started a kitchen shortly after the strike began with other women from her village of Newtongrange, near Edinburgh, at the miners' welfare.

At the end of the strike, Joyce said she did not think that eating in the kitchens at the social club had done the children any harm.

If anything, they've been spoilt, because a lot of the people here tend to spoil the wee ones and give them extra pennies. It must have cost the club a fortune because it has got to the stage where they just go and help themselves to crisps. It's like a big playschool. And there have been three babies – I've watched them grow up. There's one who was nine months when he started coming here. Now he'll eat anything you give him in the kitchen. He loves it. The other two were only babies when they first came and now they are actually talking away. Their speech is perfect. It's good to watch them just walking up and getting their dinner, then coming back and sitting down and eating it. If anyone at all needs a babysitter, there's no problem. The bairns know them all and will go with them. If there is an emergency meeting there is always someone on hand. I've watched two or three of somebody else's kids and they've watched mine.

No wonder that when the strike ended the miners' wives were reluctant to go back to their old way of life. They were determined to keep the women's new solidarity together somehow.

After the strike, the kitchen stayed open for the miners who had been sacked for picket line offences by the National Coal Board, and Joyce Coutts' husband was one of them. Although the offences committed were often extremely minor, many did not get their jobs back after the strike, even though the Industrial Relations Tribunals had said they should.

Joyce said:

From the start we all took turns at coming into the kitchen to do the cooking. There were some women in the kitchen all the time. But if they needed help then anybody was ready to stand in. Even the men were taking turns. There were men peeling potatoes at night time for the meal the next day and every day they brought up food from the cellar. Everybody just mucked in, men and women.

From the beginning, she said, she had been 100 per cent behind the strike.

The biggest threat was jobs. My husband was an engineer in the Bilston colliery and had been there since he left school. So I just could nae imagine him being on the dole or anything like that because he's just not that kind, so I stood by him no matter what rough and tumbles.

He was in favour of the strike.

We sat down and talked about it the day before the strike. We just thought: well, this is it – though how long we did nae know. But there was no way we were turning back. To start with, the first time I worked in the kitchen was in the Easter break in the kids' holiday. We fed those kids for the whole fortnight they were off school.

Her little boy was three when the strike started 'and now he can practically walk to the kitchen himself. There's a lot of kids like him – wee ones – and they just toddle along to get their dinners themselves.'

Even if some fathers had returned to work, as eventually 50 per cent of the men did at Bilston Glen, the women never ignored the children.

Maybe they've had various different problems. Somebody might be hiding problems that they did nae want to discuss. Maybe it's pressure that's put a man back. It must be horrible for them to think that their kids are nae getting money or that their kids are being deprived of this and the next thing, so sometimes you can understand it.

There were some who stayed at home and did not come down to the soup kitchen.

It must have been harder. But that was their own choice. They knew they could come down. If there was a new member came in they got their dinner like everybody else. Maybe it did seem a bit clannish, because all the women were here from day one. It would seem a bit strange to a new one but after a day or so you'd be just like everyone else.

Food Parcels

The chief co-ordinator for the pits in Dulais Valley, mid-Glamorgan in Wales, was Kay Bowen, the wife of the delegate at Blaenant colliery. Her area covered four pits, which, in rural Wales, meant immense transport difficulties. The pits were in three valleys, stretching over 30 miles, with 1,080 scattered families to be fed. 'And going in at one end of the valley does not mean you can get out at the other. We drove thousands and thousands of miles,' Kay said.

A food parcel of 17 items was distributed to each family each week: cabbages, swedes, carrots, apples and oranges, a loaf of bread, a pint of milk, six eggs, a tin of meat, a tin of beans, half a pound of margarine, cereal, a packet of biscuits, a tin of soup and potatoes.

It filled two carriers and it really was not more than about two days' supply but it was all they had. We varied it, or tried to, every week. The single men were glad to get anything, but I really don't know how they managed on nothing.

Keeping warm in winter was often worse than the hunger. People were having their gas cut off for not being able to pay their bills, even though they were classified as 'in desperate need'. Families were desperate with cold. The bailiffs were in their houses taking everything to pay debts. The families in Neath and Swansea suffered the worst, far out from the pits and isolated from other miners.

Some of the groups ruled that if a wife was working, the family did not get a parcel. But our group didn't. Often we had to persuade people to ask for help – not to go back to work at the pit where there was no one to help them, but to let their communities help them if they got into real trouble. When they were very proud it was very difficult.

In the end, we used wood for heating. The Forestry Commission leased us some woodland, and we chopped the trees to make fires and took round the logs. That saved us.

Two men went back to work after coming to us for help, and we'll never speak to them again. No one will ever talk to them. If the pit closes, it will be due to them. The very first man to go back even had a working wife and grown children. The other men now ignore him. The scab lorries which were used to fetch the coal to the power stations – no one will use them now.

The Bowens have four children, aged between 3 and 12. Kay had been organising the distribution of food parcels while her husband was away for weeks and months at a time, fund-raising and public speaking. Although Blaenant produces power station coal, the men were told it was non-productive and over-manned. It needed investment and new machinery.

'Since the strike, women are asking more questions about mining, learning more, and getting more involved,' said Kay. At first she had found it difficult without her husband, with four children and the support groups to organise, but had learned to cope in a way she had not expected. She also went off speaking while their father looked after the children, and had been on platforms in Derbyshire, London and in Ireland. Kay had never thought she would dare to speak in public, but now she did not find it difficult. 'And I'd thought I'd never be able to give orders or ask people to do things. But I've found I like leadership and being in charge. I've changed, like all the other women, and I'll never be able to go back to how I was before.'

The only money the Bowen family had to live on during the strike was £27 per week plus £27 for family allowances. But she had found she could manage. 'You knew where you were, you knew exactly how much money you were going to have, and you just had to plan. But knowing so exactly how much money you had meant you *could* plan. The worst thing was always having to say no to the children when they asked for treats. But it was a way of life. We all helped each other and you got used to it.'

She also understood the attitude to scabs. 'We were fighting for those scab lorry drivers' jobs as well. If that colliery closes, all the jobs dependent on it will go.'

Changing Roles

Men and women learned about each other's strengths as well as weaknesses. The miners cleaned houses and looked after children and cooked as a matter of routine – something that most of them had never done before.

Pauline Radford from Blidworth said:

> I think the men are becoming more aware of what the women are doing gradually, and I think the women are getting on better with their husbands because we're learning a lot more about politics and things going on in the country and the whole world. Instead of just talking about the kids and the house and what you've done during the day, you've got a wide range of things that you've learned that you can talk about.

One of the deepening divisions as the strike went on was between the women who still saw their lives as only fitting around men's lives, and the rest who didn't feel they had to make excuses for becoming active in politics in a way their mothers might not have approved of.

One striking miner in his mid-thirties, at Maerdy colliery in the Rhondda valley in Wales, put the position very eloquently just after the strike had ended.

> I should say about 90 per cent of the women have changed since the strike started. Before, you felt you were just the person who went home on a Friday night with the pay packet. There was nothing to look forward to, nothing to talk about. You just thought about how you could manage to pay the bills. Now we read the newspapers, think a lot about world affairs we see on television, and think maybe we can change things. It's different from the 1930s. Men and women have been in it together. When that strike was over, the miners crawled back to work on their knees. This time we marched back with the women at the head of the march, singing. We

didn't feel beaten.

Doreen Humber thought the men had been shocked by what was going on at first. Probably that was true, but only because tradition and conditioning had taught them to be shocked.

Susan Petney of Blidworth explained:

We are sort of re-educating them slowly. They are not liking it a lot. You see, we've all been brought up in a certain mould, especially the miners. They've been brought up that they are the men, the bread winners – and that women should stay at home and be seen and not heard. But slowly they are coming round to it. They don't call us 'ladies' any more. They call us women. That's a start.

In Derbyshire, the organisation of the women's support groups was born during Tony Benn's by-election campaign before the strike. And they had Betty Heathfield, wife of the General Secretary of the NUM, who is a first rate organiser and diplomat.

In the strike headquarters at Chesterfield, the miners treated Betty Heathfield and her companions with a special respect. There was no problem about who made the tea. The men were only too willing to make it for the women – they seemed to take a positive pleasure in doing so. The miners also made up the food parcels and packed the baby food and tinned soups.

If Betty Heathfield thought something was important, and she was supported by Peter Heathfield, then everyone accepted it. Men carrying children, taking them to and from school, queuing up for food parcels, doing the shopping if there was any money, making the tea and the sparse meals became commonplace.

And the women's social life changed, as they became used to going out on their own. One Scots wife said that before the strike she would never have gone out with another woman.

Now, after the strike, I'll go out on a night out with the girls.

I'll go out with the miners' club bar stewardess which I would never have done before. I used to totally disagree with that. It's annoying some of the men as a matter of fact.

Previously, miners' wives had been first and foremost someone's property. They might know a lot about coalmining, but it just wasn't done to have friendships with other men – that would have been a breach of the husband's or boyfriend's territorial rights. This changed, too, with the crisis of the strike.

Before, if I was with my husband and one of his workmates came by, he'd just say 'hello', and that was that. Now he will sit down and have a chat with me.
Some of the men, my husband's friends and that, they've even remarked on that, that before I was just a wife, but that now I sit down and ask how things are going. They think this is a better way. A lot of the wives aren't so quiet now. I think now the roles are changing, the men are staying in with the kids and the women are out.

Some men found it very difficult to get used to the fact that it was not them but their wives who would be rolling merrily through the door after midnight, the better for a few drinks after the evening meeting and full of stories about their successes.
But no one felt like discouraging the women – not while they were scoring such a triumph in bringing support from professional groups and other women on to the side of the miners, and raising enough money to keep the strike going.
All this proved to the women that a social life need not be dependent on money and men. When the miners had plenty of money, their wives rarely went out. It took the strike, and getting to know people who wanted to help, to give them an organised social life.
The bar stewardess in Scotland – who had enjoyed the nights out with the women and had presumably paid for them – was disappointed when the strike ended and she did not see them

any more. 'She's been quite involved in the strike. She's feeling it as well, beause she is thinking that once all the men are back the wives will stop coming.'

Everyone seemed to be developing new talents. At its best, the new system worked as a model of what the first socialist pioneers of the last century had dreamed about. Men and women swopped roles, without even pausing to think about what they were doing. A miner might be away for a week, touring, public speaking, raising funds, or on the picket line. When he returned he would look after the children, while his wife would go off as guest of a local town which had 'twinned' with the local pit, or further afield.

The pattern of life did not always go as smoothly as that of course. There were likely to be many problems. A child would drop behind at school, or someone would be ill. The point, however, was that for the first time ever the women were having the benefits not only of an organised support system, which came to their rescue at any time, but also of husbands treating them with a totally new respect.

The miner's practical approach to domestic life had its funny side. A miner's wife in Nottingham told how her husband, a striker from the Blidworth pit, solved the Hoover problem.

Pauline [another member of the support group] lives next door to me and both our Hoovers were broken. My husband's an electrician at the pit, so he made one decent one out of two. But they're falling out now over whose turn it is to have the Hoover, and if one of them hasn't emptied the bag, they're falling out with each other about that, too.

Family Upheavals

During the strike family patterns were changing. The family structure had to change – or break under the strain. Betty Heathfield, in the autumn of 1984, said, 'Each family will be having to sort itself out. Let's say that there are lots of discussions and arguments going on up and down the country. The women have got the confidence to do a lot of things they haven't done before.'

And in many cases men did not like it, even though some did. One wife of a northern miner told of the appalling difficulties of the last months of the strike, after nearly a year of poverty, hunger and debt.

In the last couple of months I felt I just had to get away from it all. I'd been secretary of the women's support committee. I felt as though I had cracked up, as though the walls were closing in on me. My husband and I started arguing, which we'd never done before, never. We split up and went back and split up. It was only for a day or so, because we knew there was nothing really wrong with our marriage.

I'm still behind him, really. The strike has affected everybody. It's not nice for the kids to see you arguing; it's not healthy for them, so we decided to split up.

When I gave up the committee I stopped working altogether. I stopped working in the soup kitchen. It felt funny. I had been working from day one, or near enough, and this was going on for the ninth month, and my home . . . it was OK, like, but you never got anything done because you were in the soup kitchen from, say, 10 in the morning to 3 in the afternoon, then the kids were back from school, then it was teatime, then it was seven and it was bath time, it was just a continual day, never ending. I was getting to the stage where I couldn't sleep at night, thinking, what have I got to do tomorrow? I had bad headaches and the doctor said it was stress, so I packed it in. Everything just got on top of everything else, and then we had the one big argument and that was it.

We'd split all the jobs down the middle, looking after the kids and the house. I think what maybe got to my husband was that I was out nearly every night. I was busy going to rallies and meetings. Obviously you had to be dressed properly – you were either talking at meetings or working in the soup kitchen. It was a big strain. But there's no way I would have changed it. I wouldn't have changed anything – nothing – I couldn't have changed a thing. I'll never settle down again, never. I used to be quiet, you know. I never used to bother anybody. But now I can't settle down again; I have to be active. I'll need to start working or something.

Her children were seven and four, and so long as they were looked after it did not worry them that their mother was out a lot. What seemed to have caused the strain that could not be borne by their marriage was that her husband had been sacked from his job for a minor picket line offence. Being sacked by the NCB meant being sacked for life, as they had a monopoly on the pits. A miner could be fined a small sum for a small offence. Then, in a short time, the letter would arrive giving him the sack from the pit. If the family lived in an NCB house it meant that they could lose their home as well.

This woman was shattered that after 10 years the marriage had blown up. 'It'll take months for us to really get back together. I see him. We talk; we go out for a drink – it's like we're married but not living in the same quarters. I'm not doing anything more than that; my heart won't take it.'

She did not think any of the women would go back to being housewives.

Some of them will have more kids and they'll have to settle down. But the ones who don't want any more kids, a lot of them will want a job. That's the next best thing to what we've been doing.

I think I would take up a job. When I got married, I got married to be a housewife and look after my kids, and be there when he went to work and came home from work. But now I can't settle down to being that again. It was a boring life, it really was. I said to my mother I don't know how I've done that and she understands because she knows what we're going through in the strike. I couldn't go back to being what my mother is, just a housewife. It's right dull, Hoovering, ironing and washing every day. My mother thinks I've changed – she's a miner's wife and she knows. She thinks I'm awfully strong-minded. I used to just accept everything. Now I'll fight to the end – the strike's brought that out in me. If I've got an argument, I'll fight it as long as I know I'm right. I'll fight it.

In many places in Britain, especially Scotland, it had become easier for women to find a job than for men. They would work part-time for low pay and they were adaptable – and that was what employers were now looking for.

Some families lived entirely on the women's earnings. One miner in Chesterfield was living on the grant of £1,400 his wife was getting in her final college year of training as a youth and community worker. Their children were 14, 11 and 7, so they were living on very little. What view did he have of human nature in December 1984?

Better. Ann's college students, her friends, are fantastic. They gave us food parcels and toys for the younger children. Before the strike I always thought no one wanted to talk to me because I was a miner. Ann went to college as a mature student, but we didn't mix with people she met there. Now, we go to dinner parties and ordinary parties and everyone seems to want to talk to me. They want to know about the pits. The professors and lecturers actually regard me as normal. They've found out miners are just like other people, though they didn't used to think so before. My opinion of human nature has improved.

While she was at college, he looked after the children. He was a large and articulate man. 'It goes all right. I don't mind. I like taking them swimming and going out with them.'

Kate Whiteside, the organiser of the support group at Chesterfield, had strong views about the new role of women.

There is no way these women will put up with things as they were before. There is going to be some turmoil in the home before things are sorted out, but already men are doing the housework in the Derbyshire communities, and looking after the children, and it is working OK. Women are organising meetings, speaking, doing everything – plus getting the food and going on the picket line and often doing a job as well. This strike has been the biggest political and social education the working-class woman has ever had – they are finding out about themselves and what they can do.

Babs Williams, the leader of the Rhondda women at Maerdy in Wales, put the position very simply: 'We have shaken men. Men thought we were content with our lot. Now they realise that a woman is not just a wife in the house; there's something else in the house.'

3.
Coal and Greenham Common

Both the miners and their wives had seen the false logic of closing pits, which put men out of work and which led to dependence on the potentially disastrous nuclear power. The political whims of one short generation of politicians were casually tearing the mining communities' lives and history to pieces. It could scarcely be said to be in the national interest. About 50 per cent of the population of England and Wales and over 70 per cent of the people of Scotland are against nuclear power. The huge investments required in construction and maintenance render nuclear power stations scarcely more economic than pits.

Economists have calculated these costs, but the Tory government has ignored the results of their calculations. For the government, 'clean' nuclear power, with its deadly unseen hazards for unborn generations, appears to be vastly preferable to radical, dirty miners opposed to the establishment and most of what the Conservative Party stands for.

It was the nuclear issue that first brought the miners and the the Greenham women peace campaigners together.

The Edinburgh Gala

Two Greenham women were invited by the Scottish NUM to

speak at the Scottish miners' gala in Edinburgh in the early summer of 1984. This is the most important miners' gathering of the year in Scotland, which all mining families attend and to which they bring picnics which they eat on the slopes of Edinburgh's mountain, Arthur's Seat.

Before they spoke the miners heard Bruce Kent, then general secretary of the Campaign for Nuclear Disarmament and the guest of honour. The theme of the gala, 'Jobs with Peace', had been decided before the strike. Bruce Kent's speech established the link which joined all protesters against nuclear weapons to the miners striking against pit closures. The government was seeking to take Britain down the dangerous and costly road of a nuclear energy programme, he said, though in the United States a similar programme had been abandoned because of doubts about its safety. 'But to do that they have first to break you, the miners,' he told his audience. ' "Uneconomic" is the phrase they use. This is the economics of Toy Town.' He angrily attacked the Cabinet decision, made in 1979, to embark on a nuclear programme in order to end the country's dependence on coal and oil.

The two Greenham women spoke against nuclear power – which provides plutonium for weapons – and in favour of coal. Those who are familiar with the mining communities can understand how strange it was to see two women on the traditional all-male miners' platform – ordinary women, without make-up and hairstyles, speaking with total confidence about their ideas. Their confidence was passed to the women in the support groups who heard them. The Greenham women's influence was soon to be strong in the women's support groups and consequently on the whole course of the strike.

The Scottish electricity grid, which already had a surplus of energy and received nearly half of its electricity from nuclear power, was helping to keep the English consumers free of power cuts during the strike. In addition, at Torness, on the east coast, an advanced gas-cooled reactor plant was being constructed, due to be in commission by 1987. This, said the NCB, would avoid 'excessive demands' for coal at a time when it could be difficult to meet such demands economically from Scottish sources. It was a ten-year multi-million pound project and, at the demand of local people, a public inquiry was held into the hazards of moving the nuclear waste from the plant across country to Sellafield. The building of the Torness nuclear power station seemed to confirm the miners' view that most of them would become dispensable in the Scottish coalfields by the 1990s.

Support from Greenham

The support Greenham women gave to the miners did not come without many arguments among themselves.

The women at Greenham who had come from the mining communities – and these were some of the first Greenham marchers from Wales – readily accepted the miners' case against pit closures, having already made the connections between nuclear power and its risks and the need for alternative fuel.

They had been the first to go to prison for protesting against nuclear weapons and they were impatient with the hesitation of others at the beginning of the strike who were doubtful as to whether keeping pits open agreed with their 'green' view of society. Coal was 'unecological', they said. No one should be asked to do filthy and dangerous jobs underground. Like most people with no direct experience, their knowledge of miners was mainly culled from literature: the novels of D.H. Lawrence and the writings of George Orwell. The women had grown up in the belief that the collieries were places from which you tried to release people, not keep them underground.

They did not know then of modern engineering techniques and mechanical devices which made the newest pits cleaner and safer, or of recent scientific advances which have enabled the pollution of coalmining to be removed, or of the many new uses for coal.

Greenham Common is a lively and knowledgeable debating

forum, the edge sharpened by the razor-sharp wire a few feet from the campfires and the troops who listen in with their rifles loaded.

It was when the injustices in the mining villages began to be revealed that the women started to unite in wanting to help the women's support groups. Nevertheless, even after the invitation came from the Nottinghamshire miners to visit the support groups, Greenham women were not wholeheartedly accepting the miners' cause.

By the summer of 1984, however, as striking miners began to claim wrongful arrest and injuries by the police, and the mining communities were suffering from illness and malnutrition, the Greenham women had actively started to support them. Coaches were hired to take them to the picket lines in Wales and Nottinghamshire, where the women tried to persuade the miners to adopt non-violent tactics. They were by now for the most part absolutely convinced of the rightness of the miners' case.

Not many women in the Nottinghamshire support groups – at Clipstone, incidentally, they were careful to the last to call themselves the Ladies Support Group – had known much about the Greenham women before the strike.

They would arrive at support centres unexpectedly and on impulse, in the way they did most things. A group would suddenly appear at a miners' welfare club, dressed in their warm, practical and comfortable clothes, which, however, appeared strange to the miners' wives, and smelling of woodsmoke. They would then start to talk. Anxious as they were not to intrude into the intensely private world of mining communities, they were nevertheless determined to help if they possibly could.

The strike had been going only five weeks when the first Greenham women arrived in Blidworth in Nottinghamshire. One woman said:

They just walked in and everyone was asking who they were, you know, because they were dressed like Greenham

Common women have to dress, and we're not used to that. I said, 'Well, can you tell me who you are?' and they gave those funny, disguised names they give themselves, and said, 'We're from Greenham Common.' I said 'Oh' and I thought Oh, dear, what do we talk about? Because it was all still new to us. So I sat down and talked to them. We went on talking for about three hours and we thoroughly enjoyed talking to them, and when they left they said they'd enjoyed it too, because they realised that because of our strike they are not on their own, now. The miners' strike has proved that there are other strong women around the country, who can do what we've done. It did us all good to talk to each other.

The Greenham women pointed out that women had a choice whether to go to Greenham or not. But the miners' wives had no such choice. They were in the strike without choice, 24 hours a day, up to their necks in it. They said they were going to help all they could. Co-operation between the two groups of women went on right through the strike.

They would sit down with the women and start to chat to them. They had plenty of practical advice to offer about how to survive the lack of food, how to keep out the cold, and displayed an immense sang froid about how to cope with policemen.

Soon Greenham women produced their own badge 'At Greenham or on the picket line'. For most of the summer of 1984 they were picketing with the miners' families.

It was not funds, or food, or any other material items which were important – though these were in fact given to the miners' support groups. It was the Greenham women's confidence of being able to accomplish things which was their most important donation to the miners' wives.

Fifteen foot high barbed wire? No problem. No food? Nothing to keep out the cold? No hot water? No friends? Hostile police? The Greenham women had been through three winters of this, and worse. Here they were, seemingly cheerful and jokey, as they had been when they were on one of their unconventional bids to attract attention to themselves and their opposition to nuclear weapons . . . scaling a wall at peace talks in Geneva, perhaps, or dancing round a captured KGB guard in a Moscow camp site and covering him with peace badges, or demonstrating at the Berlin Wall. They seemed to the women in the support groups almost totally fearless, and as ingenious and ingenuous as a Resistance army.

Visits to Greenham

On a hot July afternoon, tea was offered to three Nottingham-shire miners who had decided to visit Greenham.

The miners were brought to Greenham by women Labour Party activists who were taking them to London on visits to raise funds for the Nottinghamshire miners' families. They had said they would like to see the Greenham base and women protesters. Most of the information miners had about Greenham had been gleaned only from the malicious coverage in the *Sun* newspaper.

Sarah Hipperson, an ex-magistrate living at Greenham, was appalled by the miners' stories. They told of sudden and unexplained arrests when walking outside their own houses, of being held for hours in police cells without being able to make a phone call, of people being beaten up and bundled into vans who had not committed any crime. They were stories familiar to journalists covering the strike in the mining areas.

The Greenham women advised the miners of what they should do. They had evolved tactics for dealing with snatch arrests. For example, other women would form a circle round the one arrested and start singing. It was not a tactic miners were likely to adopt, but Sarah Hipperson started taking them step by step through the processes of law leading to the magistrates' court, outlining their legal rights and telling them what they could legally object to. She emphasised that they must stand up for these rights, and the women once more urged them that if they considered themselves to be not guilty, they should plead not guilty, and refuse to pay their fines.

Wood was collected for the fire, the kettle finally boiled, and the miners were given tea. They said it was the best they had ever tasted, and asked the women to visit Nottinghamshire.

Nottinghamshire miners' wives started to go to Greenham in coaches. The sudden awareness of the likelihood of nuclear war and what it could do to them brought fresh worries.

One woman told of her first visit to Greenham and its nine miles of barbed wire fencing, the watchtower and soldiers and police guarding the Cruise missiles in their silos, and the constant patrols.

I went to walk round on my own and see it all. It really got to me. It made me sick. When I got home late at night there was the programme on television, the film about when the Bomb went off. My husband was watching it and he said, 'This is a fantastic film'. I watched it for a bit and then I snapped at him. He just saw it as entertainment. He said: 'Is this what happens when you clear off for the day?' I said: 'You've just watched that film and told me what you think of it, but I've just been where all that is, and to come home from seeing that and to watch it on television, it makes me feel sick. It's not something you can push to the back of your mind. It's something that can happen and is there, and that is why I feel so uptight about it all.'

Another woman said: 'We didn't even know before about them dropping test bombs in the Pacific. The ones who do it are all safe – they've got their bunkers – but we don't matter.'

Doreen Humber said:

Sometimes I look at my little lad; he's five, and I think, 'I wish I'd never had him'. That's how it makes me feel. Because I think if we lose what we have in this world, either by making nuclear bombs or putting people on the scrapheap, if we lose this fight, there is nothing to bring up kids for. I've got a grandchild, too, being born any time. And it frightens me to death that that child is coming into this world as it is now. That's why we've got to stick it out and try to do something. I can't think how anybody can be so stupid as to do what they are doing to this country. We've got to stick it out.

'Greenham is suffering from the police, like us,' said Kay Sutcliffe from Kent. 'They have a tremendous fight on their hands but they can't be pushed into the background now. Greenham are fighting for us all. Hopefully we'll take another bus to visit Greenham and other groups might come with us.' (This they did and so kept their promise.)

Greenham Women and the Miners

Though the Greenham women formed a strong bond between themselves and the women in the mining communities, the friendliness never really extended to the miners themselves.

The miners had most of what Greenham considered to be the usual male faults – miners were inclined to be violent and they wanted women kept in their place. Nor did the miners understand Greenham women. 'Surely it's not safe for them here?' said one miner arriving at Greenham, not realising the very thin ice he was treading on, or how the very fact of being a man would normally have disqualified him even from being there. 'They need us to protect them; I wouldn't trust those American troops. Maybe some of us should come down and have a go at them?' he continued, watching a loud-mouthed US sergeant driving through the camp in his Cadillac on the way to the main road to Newbury. Nobody replied.

The gulf between the Greenham women and the miners was wide and unbridgeable, and the pact for the duration of the strike was like an uneasy wartime alliance.

The miners themselves were disinclined to listen to the women's talk of non-violence.

Nor did they relish the idea of refusing to pay fines and going to prison as a consequence, as the Greenham women had done and were doing. With thousands of miners and some of their wives being arrested the prisons would soon be full, the Greenham women pointed out. The authorities would then have to take notice. Already courts were sitting into the early hours of the morning to hear the pickets' cases in Nottinghamshire.

The Greenham women were not able to make headway with the miners in their belief that violence should not be returned with violence. Their own non-violent demonstrations followed the traditional method of peace protest movements.

Non-violence had been used as a civil disobedience tactic in Britain when Bertrand Russell had formed the Committee of 100, the militant arm of CND in the early 1960s. As in West Germany, the United States and other countries where people were engaged in non-violent protest against nuclear weapons, the protesters in Britain would simply sit down in the road and refuse to move. Greenham women improved on this tactic by climbing over the wire fencing round the base and dancing on top of the missile silos. Once – illegally – inside the base, as well as sitting down and walking around the military establishments, they would roller-skate, drive vehicles, scrawl peace signs anywhere possible, scale the air control tower to put peace signs in the office, camp out secretly inside the base, and sit down in the road whenever the Cruise missile launchers were brought out of the base to lumber clumsily around the country lanes surrounding the Greenham base. But all the protests were essentially non-violent.

Once or twice, the Greenham women managed to persuade the miners and their support groups to try sit-down demonstrations. But at Port Talbot in Wales, this brought about disastrous consequences. Pickets, being driven on from behind by the police, fell down over the men in front of them who were staging a sit-in on the ground, and this caused chaos and injuries which were worse than they might have been had the sit-in not taken place.

Another serious attempt at a sit-down protest was organised, also with disastrous consequences, at the end of August by

Dave Douglas, the Hatfield Main delegate in Yorkshire. A strong personality, he was trusted, and he persuaded the pickets that a change in tactics was needed. But the outcome was very unlike any experience at Greenham. It was described by Lynn Clegg, of the Hatfield Main Women's Support Group.

> The lads got battered to bits. We'd been there all day, watching the scabs going in, with no trouble. Police knew we were going to do something. Dave got everyone sat down in the middle of the road. The lads sat down for five or ten minutes talking, but I was on the wall and could see the police and what was going to happen. The atmosphere was electric; you could tell something terrible was going to happen. The lads couldn't see because they were sitting down, but the inspector said something and within 30 seconds the police just charged in riot gear. It was absolutely terrifying. The lads didn't even have a chance to see or get up. The police went in with batons, just hitting anybody and one lad was put in intensive care. It was the worst day we ever had at Hatfield.

In Scotland, a more successful attempt had been made in May by miners travelling by coach from Polmaise colliery, near Stirling, and other pits to picket the lorries taking imported coal into the Ravenscraig steel works to replace the Scottish coal.

Led by John McCormack, the Polmaise delegate, the pickets, stopped by the police before they reached Glasgow, refused to turn back. Instead, they got out of the coaches and sat down in a chain across the road.

There were nearly 300 miners, and each one had to be lifted into police vans and taken to Glasgow to be detained and questioned. Local politicians raised a rumpus about civil liberties, because the men had been arrested without having committed any crime, they said. It was an example of the value of peaceful resistance. After a time, however, the miners and the miners' wives who picketed with them in Scotland stayed on their own side of the Border and their influence was lost to the English and Welsh mining communities.

The Greenham women feared that the miners might return violence with violence. Their suspicions were proved to be correct.

In non-violent protest, protesters go limp, making it extremely hard for the police to move them. Non-violent tactics have to be learned. It is difficult not to retaliate if brutal treatment is received. Concentration and discipline are necessary.

The miners had not been schooled in these tactics, nor were the majority much interested in them, anyway. Their physical strength was what mattered to them, and this they were proud of. A Scottish miner, describing one of the first picket line clashes with police in Yorkshire, said: 'The police got in a great V shape and pushed and pushed until we couldn't move or breathe. Then this policeman took a kick at me.'

'What did you do?' I asked.

'Kicked him back, of course. Harder.'

Carry Greenham Home

The influence of the first women marchers to Greenham from Wales was strong in the Welsh coalfield throughout the strike, even among women who had never been to Greenham and probably never would. And there were many women from Wales who felt a deep empathy with Greenham. Glenys Kinnock, for instance, was a familiar visitor at Greenham, both before and during the strike.

Greenham women staged many demonstrations outside power stations and even electricity showrooms in places where nuclear power was extinguishing jobs and causing local anxieties as the power stations were constructed and the reactors moved into place.

This was one of the reasons why there were fewer women at Greenham Common itself during 1984 and the early part of 1985.

The miners' strike had helped to move their ideas outwards from nuclear weapons to other areas of a sick society which leaned on these weapons for its protection. Now they were working against pit closures, for prison reform – having tasted overcrowded and inhuman prison conditions – and also unemployment.

After the strike had ended the women went back to Greenham and to their watch over the Cruise missiles, attempting to block the missile launchers' movements in and out of the base. Some of the miners' wives and their families, and even the miners themselves, still support them. They hire coaches and go to Greenham, and the links have been maintained. Like very many other women all over the world, the Women Against Pit Closures are also Greenham women, a description which applies to a way of thinking and, sometimes, a particular lifestyle. 'Carry Greenham Home' means what it says.

4.
On the Picket Line

Many of the miners did not like to see women pickets, certainly not on the same picket as themselves. One miner in the Rhondda said: 'It's too much if you see the police getting at your women. It just makes the whole thing more difficult if they're there.'

It was Anne Scargill and members of the Barnsley Women Against Pit Closures who led the way in militant picketing by women. She had appeared several times on the picket lines in Nottinghamshire and was arrested at Silverhill colliery, with the prosecution saying that she clung to the perimeter fence after police had told her to move. But she and three other women, Lyn Hathaway, Liz Hollis, an organiser of the Nottinghamshire Women's Support Group, and Audrey Moore, also from Nottingham, were all cleared of causing obstruction. The magistrate dismissed their case, which did not actually come to court until the following October.

At Staveley colliery in Derbyshire, where half the pits were threatened by closure, a miner looked after his four children under the age of 6 when his wife was held on picketing charges. He was told that the charges would be dropped against her and that she could come back home again – so long as he went back to work. He refused.

Police Tactics

Riots and violence were breaking out in Yorkshire, Derbyshire and the Nottinghamshire borders. Hunger and exhaustion were taking their toll in anger and violence. Stress was growing in both the pit and police communities, living as they were in camps far away from home.

The rest of the country, of course, was going about its normal life. There was little support for the NUM from the other unions. There were queues at the airports in the north and south of Britain for package holidays. People were concerned about getting a job and somewhere to live. They were trying not to think about the miners. For the striking miners and their families it was rock-bottom time. After five months of soup kitchens it looked like the end. But this was in fact far from the case.

Nothing stands still. The strike was moving towards a state of virtual civil war, and the police were ready for this. They had been training to contain what they described as 'urban unrest' for a number of years.

The then Commissioner at New Scotland Yard, Kenneth Newman, had led the Royal Ulster Constabulary in Northern Ireland. He had moved from there to take charge of the Bramshill staff training college for senior officers in the south of England. The Yard was seriously preparing for a situation where the violence in Northern Ireland might be duplicated in the mainland. There had been the Toxteth riots, the Brixton riots – and now it was to be the miners, trying to overthrow authority. The government were seizing the opportunity to put down these renegades, once and for all.

On the whole, the Commissioner was in favour of the new riot weaponry with which the police were being equipped. He thought that, though the use of riot squads should be seen by chief constables to be a last resort, they were better and more easily controlled than the alternative, which he described as 'a lot of constables charging about'.

Nevertheless, from his point of view, the operation during

the miners' strike was a failure. The idea had been to improve methods of co-ordination to contain disorder without having to resort to weaponry. The co-ordination came through the police national reporting centre, but in the end only succeeded in making areas of the country look like a police state.

The riot shields and weaponry proved to incite rather than control people who were already desperate, hungry and suffering from a burning sense of grievance. In addition, picketing was too often an opportunity for the strikers to drink. It was an explosive mixture – and it exploded.

Some senior policemen resented being forced to use criminal law on behalf of situations created by the Tories. They thought civil law should have been used to enforce the anti-trade union laws the government had passed. When, at the beginning of the strike, police had stopped Kent miners in the Dartford tunnel, and had turned them back on the thin excuse that they *might* be going to commit a crime hundreds of miles away, police even then felt they were being unfairly used for political ends. The end result could only be to damage civil liberties – which the police were supposed to protect. John Alderson, formerly head of the Devon and Cornwall police and an ex-assistant Commissioner at New Scotland Yard, a pioneer of community policing, pointed out, after the strike had ended, that 10,000 miners had been arrested during the strike, hundreds imprisoned, but not one policeman even disciplined, let alone charged. Could anyone seriously think the violence had been all one sided, when the police had helmets and riot shields, horses and truncheons, and the miners only T-shirts and jeans?

Hatfield Main

Summer in the Yorkshire coalfield in 1984 was probably the nearest England had come in sight of civil war since 1926. Then the NUM pulled back the pickets from confrontation and people who had been against the miners because of the violence started supporting them with funds. The Women Against Pit

Closures redoubled their fund-raising efforts and a march of the women was staged in London in August.

Hatfield Main had its worst day at the end of the month, when the miners staged a peaceful sit-down demonstration.

> They went in with batons, hitting anybody. We've got photographs. That was our worst day. We took lads to hospital with really bad injuries. It was terrible. We were right upset. The first two scabs who'd gone into work that day wouldn't go back after that. We never had any more scabs. So the police moved over to Armthorpe.

Such was the description by one miner, seven months after the strike had ended.

The women, too, described that day at Hatfield. 'The worst day at Hatfield was in August, when the first scabs went in to work. All the village came out that day. There was a police charge and one of the strikers was taken into intensive care.'

Women and the Violence

Police said to one of Betty Heathfield's picket group in Derbyshire: 'You women cause more havoc on the picket line than anyone else.' They took this as a compliment. Indeed, the women were proving themselves to be fearless when they saw people being roughed up by the police. At Staveley, when women pickets saw a man on the ground vomiting as he was beaten by police and dragged across the road, women ran across and managed to stop them. Then they covered him up and sent for an ambulance. 'You can tell there's trouble when they adjust their chin straps – you know they're going to come straight at you with their truncheons, arresting people just anyhow.'

Brenda Greenwood was arrested at Ollerton colliery, where a Yorkshire picket, Davey Jones, had died during the picketing. She was the first woman in the strike to be arrested and jailed for obstruction and threatening behaviour likely to cause a breach of the peace. In her own words, what she actually did was to stand near Ollerton colliery and say to the scabs 'You're earning blood money. Men have lost their lives for your jobs.'

Brenda's prison experience brought another dimension to the growing awareness among the women's support groups of the darker side of society. At her trial she conducted her own defence and won her case on 19 February 1985. Before the case came to court and regardless of whether she was innocent or guilty, she was on remand in prison.

In the book *Striking Women*, published by Pluto Press, she writes:

> I was arrested and taken to Risley remand centre for seven days. It was a miserable, nasty experience. The worst thing about it was the strip search. When you go in you have to strip off entirely and are taken into a room with three or four women prison warders. They run their hands over your body, look into your mouth, under your feet, under your arms, everywhere. They are continually worried about drugs being smuggled in and out. Then you go into another room where there is a nurse or matron type and they have a big iron chair. The seat of the chair is on a level with this woman's face and you had to get up on it. There were two bars going out from this chair with two loops on the end and you had to put your legs on that. You can imagine what the search was. When you don't know what to expect, it's so degrading . . . and so unnecessary.

She said that for the best part of the week she was locked up for most of the time. On the first day she had to clean the cell out and then clean the landing, the washroom and the toilets. Someone told her later in the day that she did not really have to do all this, so she asked the prison officer what her rights were concerning this heavy work. The officer told her she need not do the work, but that if she refused she would be locked up all the time. 'So I was – for 22 hours out of 24. We were let out for

15 minutes in the morning for breakfast, same for lunch and same at teatime. At 6.30 you were let out for a wash, then locked up for the night. I got some books out of the library and just buried myself in them and tried to forget the surroundings I was in.'

On the day she was released, she was strip searched again. Since then, the women in the miners' support groups have helped to campaign against the strip searches which women, particularly in Armagh jail, but also in prisons throughout Britain, say are used as punishments against them. And these strip searches are routine practice, often in front of male officers.

Kay Sutcliffe, the women's support group leader in Kent, said that the summer of 1984 was the worst time. 'We thought if we could get through that it would be OK but the strike could have quietly died during August.'

The women were especially vulnerable to threats by the police because of their sex. One policeman made a grab at a woman on a Nottinghamshire picket and hauled her off to the van. 'I've had my eye on you all the time and I fancy you,' he said. 'You'll be on your own in the cell later tonight and I'm coming round to visit you.' She was shivering and scared, though the threat was not carried out.

At Didcot power station, Glynnis Evans from Maerdy colliery saw her friend Mary being grabbed by the police. 'I saw what they were doing to her, pulling her arms behind her back, twisting her arms as they dragged her along.' She went to her help, shouting at the police to stop. 'Afterwards I realised I was lucky they hadn't arrested me, too.'

Her husband, John, said: 'Women shouldn't be on picket lines. The trouble is you can't see police doing things to a woman and not go to help. When you do, that makes even more trouble.'

Lynn Clegg from Hatfield Main went all over the country picketing. Sometimes she was on the same line as her husband. 'We never really thought about what might have happened to the kids if we'd both been arrested. Good friends were looking after them.'

She organised a women's picket at Calverton pit in Nottinghamshire.

We heard scabs there were working a night shift. We decided that that was a good time for women to picket, because they could get away while their husbands looked after the children.

There were 120 women and eight blokes, who drove the vans. It was really good when we arrived. The police couldn't believe it, all these women turning up. It was a great sight.

We got there first, then the women from Armthorpe, then Ollerton, South Elmsall, and from Upton and all over. The police were amazed at all these women turning up. We arrived first from Hatfield. The police were sitting in the pit sports club, drinking and chatting. When they saw us, they shouted 'drink up, lads', and came out, got on to their radios and called up reinforcements.

We went on to the side of the road leading to the pit. But they didn't want us there so they forced us all over to a piece of grass on the other side. They penned us in there by encircling us. Then, more and more police started to arrive and forced us over the road. They were hitting women. There were no holds barred; there were 13 women taken to hospital that night. It was terrifying. They got us penned in and women were passing out in the crush. More and more police circled round us. They seemed absolutely in their glory.

When they first saw us they were panicking. But when the reinforcements arrived it was different. The women were getting scared; it was getting dark but they wouldn't let us out. The only ones they would let go were the women who passed out – and only when we persuaded the police to let them through. I was thumped in the face and women were being kicked and punched. People were panicking. The police were just running into the crowd and making arrests. If anybody said a word, 'scab' or anything, the coppers dragged them out and arrested them. They were arresting people for no reason. My friend was dragged away by coppers six feet tall. She is only a five foot two, eight stone woman, and she was being arrested for no reason. I shouted and ran after to try to get her back. They were just hitting anybody.

A police officer hit me in the face. They were using obscene language, but when did you hear of a policeman being done on that charge? I was trying to stop them taking my friend away; she was screaming and kicking, but eventually she was thrown in a van with the others. Someone from behind dragged me out and away.

They wouldn't let us out until about 11 o'clock that night when all the men had gone into work. The women arrested were taken somewhere up north and kept overnight and all the next day until 4 or 5 and then released.

The women pickets returned again to Calverton. And then there were not so many police.

Perhaps they had a different sergeant. On the first night we really hadn't gone there intending to do anything to break the law. We just wanted to stand and tell the men they were wrong to be going to work. We had that right, we thought. That first time, the official picket of six got penned in the same as us women. And with 300 or so police there, there wasn't much the men could do to stop them hitting us.

Lynn and Tony Clegg, with their twin boys, lived in a plain little council house in a cul-de-sac in the village of Stainforth in South Yorkshire. They had tiny gardens at the front and wooden gates. Lynn pointed out of the window:

The police used to come along this road. You'd see whole convoys of police. When you see them invading your village it's bound to make you angry. When there was a police charge, they ran through people's houses. They terrified an old lady in Stainforth. They burst in and said: 'You've got fucking pickets in here' and smashed her door down. And she's 70 odd. She was absolutely terrified. It happened on loads of occasions in Armthorpe, smashing doors down and running through houses.

Armthorpe Colliery

At Armthorpe colliery in August 1984, a freelance photographer for the Italian press said the village looked like a Latin American state. The police had taken it over.

Police rode mounted through the village streets, beating shields like tom-toms. The violence broke out most dramatically when miners started to go back to work, won over by the financial inducements for Christmas offered by the NCB in 1984, and were met by those miners still on strike. Vehicles were overturned and set alight, while ball bearings and petrol bombs were used as weapons.

To anyone like myself, who had covered the peaceful village as a young reporter, covering pit disasters and miners' reaction to pay offers, this was a totally different experience. The village's swift transformation into a battle ground was bewildering.

Normally the village is a comfortable, homely, solid-looking place, with well cared for houses, plentiful shops and an air of modest prosperity. It was a contrast to many of the bleak and deprived mining villages in the poorer coalfields in Scotland which I had grown used to. The outburst of emotion was a clue to the bitter passions of the strike. Yorkshire people are outwardly stolid, laconic, and not easily moved. But their emotions run deep. When their armour is finally penetrated and their traditional stubbornness pierced, the passion surprises all except those who know it is there.

In a letter to the *Guardian* (August, 1984) P. Rodriguez wrote that he had seen a unit of six police cornering innocent passers-by; people mistaken for pickets being severely beaten; police 'blatantly' entering houses without any reasonable cause; housewives and children being 'inexcusably abused'. He was writing in support of an account of events in Armthorpe by a

Guardian reporter, David Hearst.

Grimethorpe Colliery

Grimethorpe colliery in Yorkshire used to be known for its brass band and mining traditions. But in the summer of 1984 Grimethorpe was the village where the strikers stoned their local police station on a Monday lunchtime. They broke into the control room at the colliery and tried to set fire to the manager's office. People watching their television screens in the south began to think there might be more to the strike than a duel for leadership between Mrs Thatcher and Arthur Scargill. Grimethorpe looked like a battle between the IRA and the RUC. The police in their riot gear were disturbing. Was Yorkshire about to turn into a second Northern Ireland?

The Media and NUM Reaction

Television cameras showed the miners hurling bricks, setting fire to buildings and kicking policemen. They rarely showed the police actions which had provoked these reactions – because the cameras were almost invariably behind police lines. While the union leaders were, therefore, understandably hostile to the media, however mistaken this attitude might have been, the police, in contrast, were helpful. They gave information to the media about where trouble on the picket lines was likely to break out (in this connection, it was generally believed that strike committee telephones were tapped by the police) and, after the picketing confrontation had taken place, the police were the only people who would give a version of events and the number of arrests in time for the early news deadlines. Similarly, the NCB had courteous press officers always on call to give statistics of how many miners were going into work – their version of the NUM's actions – and how much damage was being done to neglected pit faces by the strikers' actions. There was no admission of any fault on the side of the establishment.

It was the NUM's own fault if it rarely received good publicity. By 1984 midsummer, even camera crews and reporters who had sympathy with the miners' case were ready to stop reporting in protest against the miners' leaders' deliberate stirring up of resentment against them. They were a handy target for hate. Some journalists were clearly frightened of even being among miners any more, and others were scared of being arrested by mistake along with the pickets, something for which their newspaper bosses would not easily forgive them.

One miner described the situation as follows:

The police acted as though they were trying to provoke trouble in South Yorkshire. It felt like how you imagined being in Northern Ireland would be. If the trouble had gone on for one more week, there'd have been rubber bullets. That's why the union said let it alone, now.

Every day the pickets were going into Nottinghamshire, and the trouble was getting worse. After Orgreave [the coking plant in Yorkshire where 3,000 pickets were confronted by 2,000 police and Arthur Scargill was arrested] it was getting out of control. When you see police beating up friends for no reason at all, you are bound to get angry. Obviously, television didn't want to show the miners' point of view. It would have been too much in the miners' favour. They didn't want people to think the miners might be right; the government didn't want the miners to win.

The cameras were always behind police lines. They would show a load of bricks coming over and the sergeant would be shouting 'Get this on your bastard cameras'. But they didn't show the baton charge and the police kicking them all the way round the field five minutes earlier, which had started it all. They didn't show you that.

Reporters and cameramen had on a few occasions stood with the pickets and the pickets had made sure they were safe.

But the police always had their lights shining towards the cameras, so the cameramen couldn't see. And behind them would be mounted policemen charging down the street on horses, knocking people down. There were vans and horses coming down the street at Silverwood colliery, with ranks of police behind the vans and horses charging down the road at the pickets. The cameras would only show what happened afterwards, not what happened to provoke it. In the end we sent the cameras away; we said we'd had enough – they weren't showing the truth.

Another miner said:

Then it really got like Northern Ireland and, after that, the union stopped everything. They said, 'Right, picket your own bits, we don't want any more trouble whatsoever'. But we didn't agree with that. They stopped people going on pickets, but that jeopardised the official pickets and made them vulnerable. They were getting hell knocked out of them by the police all the time after that. At Hatfield Main the police shut them up in the official picket hut and left them there. But the union told us we'd have to put up with it and they didn't want any more trouble.

It seemed the union were winding the strike down from the end of November, cutting back on the pickets and saying they couldn't afford to pay them. But public support was growing right up to the last month of the strike.

The Picketing Continues

In spite of the decision taken by the NUM, the picketing carried on and, indeed, throughout the bitter winter of 1984–85, the picketing never stopped. Even while the NUM executive were secretly preparing for the end of the strike, the women were organising pickets and travelling hundreds of miles to try to stop the slow drift back to work. The return to work was never as great as the NCB figures made it out to be, but the upward trend was there, all the same. Once it had reached the halfway mark the tide had turned in favour of the NCB.

Sometimes the lads managed a little revenge.

In the snow, some young miners had made a snowman and had put a policeman's helmet on it, a helmet captured in some former confrontation.

The inspector told us to knock it down, but we wouldn't. So he said to the lad in the police landrover: 'Get that down'. So the lad drove into it. But it had been built round a concrete post. It didn't half make a mess of the landrover, and the inspector had a job explaining that away.

Monktonhall Colliery

The road to the Monktonhall pit led up the hill past a row of grey council houses. Opposite them, next to the fields, police vans waited. Outside the pit, lining the gateway, stood a row of policemen.

It had been snowing all night. In the distance, the Pentland hills were completely covered by snow. It was easy to see the pit from a distance. The winding shaft and the black slag heaps stood out clearly against the sky at noon. Finding the way to the pit was more difficult. Police cars and policemen blocked the roads around, and would let no one through except the scab miners who were going in to work the afternoon shift. The road to the pit was the only one remaining open.

Since Christmas, enthusiasm for the freezing cold and darkness of the 6 am picket had waned. It was easier to picket the afternoon shift, particularly as so many miners unable any longer to stand their families being hungry and cold had started to go back to work.

Coaches which had brought miners and their wives from coalfields far away were parked further down the road, and the men and women walked slowly up towards the pit. They came

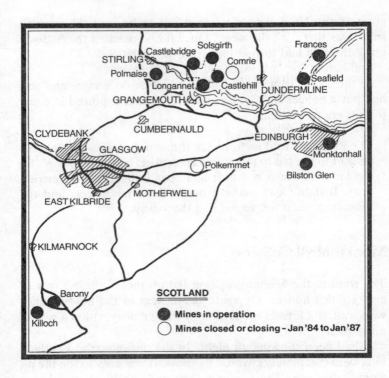

in groups. Soon there were several hundred of them. As the time for the afternoon shift drew nearer, there were nearly a thousand.

The men stood in a solid mass, right across the road. The women, a few with children, huddled against the drystone walls on each side, blackened by years of pit dust.

Nearly all the women lived in the village and had only had to walk a hundred yards or so. But a few had travelled up to 50 miles from Fife or Ayrshire in the hired coaches.

The wind was cold and the women's faces looked pinched and thin. The miners moved around, talking to each other, watching both the police and the pit.

One girl, her face bleak and exhausted, wore only a thin jacket. She kept shivering. The older women around her exchanged a few words. They climbed on to the wobbly drystone wall and kept their faces turned towards the pit. The young girl suddenly spotted her husband among the men and called to him, pushing her way through to where he stood with his mates, and took his arm. He looked embarrassed and offhand, and after a moment she went back to the wall. But later he came over and said 'Here, put this on' and took off his heavy donkey jacket, making her wear it. Then he went back to his mates. Her face suddenly lightened and she started to talk to the others.

In Scotland the daylight in winter begins to fade around 2 o'clock in the afternoon. There was a twilight feeling already about the day. In London the end of the strike was being talked about as a certainty. Yet here, up in the north of Britain, there were more pickets than there had ever been – without television cameras or any other reporters.

One of the women, older, larger, her face pale and unhealthy looking, started to talk, bitterly.

Do you think in London they've any idea at all what it's like here? Why do they think we're striking, going through all this, no food for the weans, no fires at home, nothing? They'll be sitting in their clubs with their brandy and soda, talking about us, but what do they know about what it's really like here? If they close this pit, there's no jobs at all.

Look, my husband, up there in the front, right next to the gates. He's been arrested once. He's breaking his bail, he was told not to picket the pit. But he's here. If the police decide to grab him and arrest him again, he'll go to prison. And that's a quiet man, never done anything wrong in his life, never broken the law, just doesn't want to be on the dole. We've seen what happens to people on the dole; they get depressed, cut off from other people, they go downhill.

We'll do anything to stop that happening. We've had nearly a year of this.

But the scabs, they're the worst. They're the ones stabbing us in the back. Do you know they come outside our house and shout and pester and threaten us? And a young bloke we helped at Christmas, got him clothes and food for his new baby, he's gone back to work . . . The ones who take what you've got and then go back, they're the ones I can't stand, the traitors.

Suddenly the crowd started to shift and move and the police seemed to grow into a solid wedge across the gates, several hundred strong. The buses carrying the scabs appeared, safely at the other side of the mesh gates, brought in through one of the guarded roads, and the shouting started. The women scrambled on to the wall, their faces hard and angry. 'Scab bastards!' they shouted, 'You rotten, rotten scab bastards.' Some of them were crying. Other women watched the gates anxiously to see who had been arrested this time for shouting, something the police were now treating as a criminal offence.

The coaches delivered the miners to the afternoon shift, 'the backshift', several hundred of them – and took back the early shift to their villages under police guard. The shouting went on and some struggling started near the gates, around the banners the miners were carrying.

'They're the real men, the strikers,' said one woman, taking my arm, her face desperate with the need to make somebody, anybody, understand her.

They are the best workers, the face workers, the real workers, the brave ones. The ones going back – they aren't men. They're weak, some of them drink. One of them, Will, my husband, argued with the bosses for him to be kept on after they'd sacked him for drinking, and that was before the strike. These are real men, the ones here. They won't give up. They could have got redundancy money, but they won't. They care about us and the young lads who need jobs.

The buses had now gone; the men arrested were put into police vans and taken away; and the miners started going back to their coaches. Today it had been this pit village's turn for a picket; yesterday it had been Ayrshire's turn; tomorrow it would be a pit in Fife. Men were arrested. Later they would be sacked for life by the NCB.

There was no drama and no violence. No one outside the pit villages saw it because it wasn't on television, and hardly anyone reported it.

The end of the strike was just over a month away. There was no happy ending for the pit. The woman who had been worried about her husband going to prison soon after had the NCB representative at the door, asking her and her husband where they were going to find £500 arrears in rent for the house. And he was sacked, with no reprieve, for pleading guilty to charges of breaching the peace.

Polkemmet Colliery

I was standing outside Polkemmet colliery at 5 am watching the pickets.

There were Scottish MPs, the leader of the Scottish NUM, Mick McGahey, and much speechmaking after the dawn when the working miners were driven into the pit. There wasn't any violence. Some of the picketing miners said they could understand the men going back to work in fear of losing forever their redundancy payments if they did not. 'But it's selling your job and taking it away from someone else,' one said. And already, in November, the days of the strike were numbered. Even as MPs spoke in defence of the pit, where 1,400 jobs would disappear when the Scottish National Coal Board closed it, they were like most politicians in that they were out of date in their assessment of what was really going on. One miner shouted: 'The pit's closed, closed, closed. You go down there and there's water everywhere. Everywhere you look, there are "No road" signs. Don't you understand, we've lost? They've already closed it.'

The story of the pit was a familiar one, repeated many times all over Britain. The National Union of Mineworkers maintained their normal safety cover on the pits throughout the strike to stop the pits from flooding and to prevent explosions underground. At Polkemmet, however, the men had withdrawn the safety cover in protest because six strike-breakers had gone back to work, and they refused to work alongside them. In Scotland, the NCB always switched off the power when this happened 'as a safety measure' and the result was flooding. Though the miners had offered a safety team to do repair work, they had been stopped by the NCB.

The NCB said it had found 13 million gallons of water in the shafts which were inaccessible and the pit was taking two million gallons each day it was closed. Engineers said it would take six months to remove the water. Polkemmet and its village were doomed.

Polkemmet colliery was closed in June 1986.

Emley Moor Colliery

In the valleys of South Yorkshire, the early morning picketing went on right through the winter and into March, backed by trade unionists and the unemployed, as happened in other coalfields.

Two weeks before Christmas 1984 at Flockton, on the moors between Wakefield and Huddersfield, the dark country lanes were patrolled two hours before dawn by police cars, their glossy whiteness and blue flashing lights a sharp contrast to the shabby huddle of strikers and unemployed round the pit gates. I had spent my childhood in the peaceful countryside round here, and had known some of the miners at Emley Moor. Now it seemed alien.

It was not possible to go down the lane to Emley Moor colliery, which the police were protecting. Floodlights had been switched on and the pit yard looked like a film set. A semi-circle of police in yellow jackets stood across the road. A beaten-looking line of pickets stood opposite the pit, with one limp banner. (They were NUPE workers and unemployed – the striking miners were off elsewhere that day, or else still in bed.) The early morning was bitterly cold. A police motorcyclist followed my car and radioed my car number plate back to his headquarters. It was 30 years since I had last been here, and I felt angry at the way it had been taken over by the police. It used to be the most peaceful place I had ever known. But there was no point in anger. I backed into a turning, and, followed by the motorcyclist, went up the narrow road and took the lane back to the Emley Moor television mast and Kirkburton – and my old home. A feeling of unreality remained. What were they doing here, these aliens? This was my territory, my home. Why were they treating me like a suspect criminal when I had a right to see what was going on?

Links with Other Industries

Women from Yorkshire organised a picket to the Cammell Laird's Shipyard during the strike and supported the men who were staging a sit-in on the crane as a demonstration against the closure of the yard. They joined the picket line there and made links with the men who were being arrested and their families.

We just read about Cammell Laird's in the papers and saw it on television and decided to help them. We got in touch with somebody there and told them we'd like to join the picket line and they said 'Yes, great, when are you coming?'

The link with Cammell Laird was typical of the bonds the miners were forming with other industrial groups throughout the country. These were informal, and made without any encouragement from union leadership. But the step towards greater grassroots sympathy and solidarity had been taken, and neither the government nor the national trade union leadership would be able to put out the fire the miners' strike had started.

5.
Militant Solidarity

Although very different areas geographically, Maerdy colliery in the Rhondda in South Wales and the mines in Kent coalfields had a great deal in common during the strike. They were close-knit communities, so that good communication networks allowed solidarity to be built up fast. And in both areas the proportion of threatened pit closures was exceptionally high, menacing not only jobs but a whole way of life. Hence both were exceptionally militant areas.

Maerdy

Maerdy colliery was the last pit in the Rhondda, the most famous coalfield in Britain. The year following the end of the strike, it was closed for ever, having merged with Tower colliery.

During its time of private ownership, it was notorious for the despotism exercised over the workers. The original owner, Lord Rhondda, had been replaced by the National Coal Board – but the Maerdy workers reckoned that attitudes had not changed much.

'We know now where we stand in this country, and that is nowhere,' said one of the wives, in the week after the strike had ended. 'We are still the lowest of the low, at least as far as this government is concerned.'

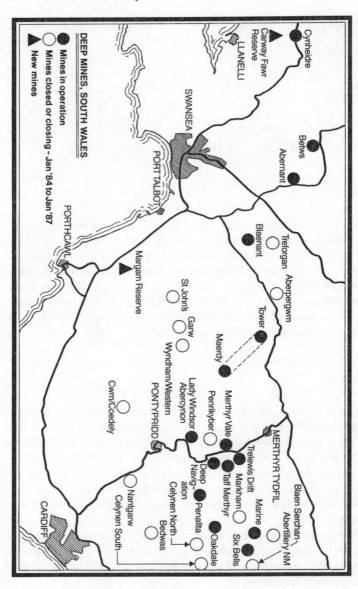

DEEP MINES, SOUTH WALES

▲ ◯ ●

● Mines in operation
◯ Mines closed or closing – Jan '84 to Jan '87
▲ New mines

It was difficult to argue with this. The Rhondda valleys stretch for 20 or 30 miles, and they are self-contained and inaccessible. There used to be 57 pits in the Rhondda, and then there was just Maerdy. And Maerdy's workforce itself had been cut from 1,400 to 750.

'People are now discovering the price of insubordination and insurrection. And boy, are we going to make it stick,' the chairman of the NCB, Ian MacGregor, was reported to have said in 1985.

This was the traditional attitude of coal-owners down the ages, and the people of the Rhondda were not surprised to come across it once again. It was what they expected.

They had seen the appointment of Ian MacGregor by the Tories as chairman of the NCB to be a long step backwards. Men would again be treated as commodities; women as cheap labour to sustain them; while the owners would react to the market, opening and closing pits and adjusting labour costs with no regard for the human beings or issues involved. This was what the strike was all about. Even the 'market economy' was not honest. Political in-fighting and power struggles often lay behind the decision to close a mine – and the miners would have no say in such decision making.

The Rhondda has the highest incidence in Wales of heart disease, arthritis, and almost every other disease you can name including, of course, 'miners' lung' (pneumoconiosis). Many houses are still without inside toilets. Few families have cars. In 20 years, 15 pits and 11,300 jobs had gone and most of the survivors are on the dole. The unemployment rate is 34 per cent. For men over the age of about 45, it is 80 per cent. The women say that 90 per cent of their children are leaving school with no prospect of a job.

Maerdy had always been the militant leader in the Welsh coalfields. Especially when all pits in the Rhondda were working. Its influence remained undimmed.

The cottages in the Rhondda go in straight lines along the narrow streets. They are old, but their paint is new. Inside there are shining, modern coal-burning stoves, new furniture, warm carpets and well-equipped kitchens. Some of the Rhondda cottages make the homes of many Londoners look bare and slovenly.

In the Rhondda, people wanted to keep security, friendships, and traditions. They did not want them wrecked. They had glimpsed a more prosperous life briefly in the mid-1970s, when the miners after the strikes of those days found themselves earning top working-class wages. These wages had at last achieved for them comfortable, pretty, well-painted homes.

The mid-1970s marked a turn in the miners' fortunes, and they were quick to build on this. But the prosperity soon started to dwindle. A way of life which had taken a hundred years to attain was now slipping away.

The women of Maerdy, who in the seventies had been given a clear vision of better times, an equality of wages and opportunity they had not known before, now knew this vision had been an illusion.

'We had our first real holiday in 1975,' said one miner's wife. 'I mean, it was the first time we had enough money to travel outside Wales, and we went to Spain. People go on about miners and how much money they had and how they never saved. But it was the first time in our lives we had even had anything that other people seemed to have – like a proper holiday in the sun with the kids, and new furniture. They say we didn't save, but we were never in debt, either.'

During the strike, other workers in Britain often used to ask why the miners had not saved while times were good so they would not be so up against it during the strike. The reason was that the miners' families were hungry for some of the material things that other workers and the middle classes took for granted. They did not want their children to miss out. They wanted books and toys, and outings and good food. They wanted warm carpets and cookers and clothes.

In Britain class prejudice shows up more than in any other way with the middle-class idea that working-class people are spendthrifts if they splash out their pay on making their own lives and their families more comfortable. Of course they want

·tty Heathfield speaking at the Miners' Rally in the City Hall,
·ffield, in November 1984. *M John, B Malone, C Pinkham*

na (left) and Bobby (right), from Bentley Women's Action
'oup, 'on the line' at Orgreave Colliery in June 1984.
issa Page/Format

OVE LEFT Women picketing Bevercotes Colliery, Nottingham,
the 10 pm Night Shift in January 1985. *Brenda Prince/Format*

LOW LEFT Ollerton Women's Support Group marches through
lerton on the weekend after the return to work in March 1985.
:nda Prince/Format

The food store at Blidworth 'soup' kitchen.
Brenda Prince/Format

BELOW RIGHT Clipstone Women's Support Group outside the hut they have used as a 'soup' kitchen for nearly a year.
Brenda Prince/Format

ABOVE RIGHT Hucknell and Linby Miners' 'soup' kitchen, run by the wives and mothers of striking miners. *Brenda Prince/Format*

ike, Diane, Tracey and Keith Lawson sold up their home in
entley, Yorkshire, in June 1984 to pay off their debts and
ntinue the strike. *Raissa Page/Format*

OVE LEFT Working on the 1984 Miners' Families Christmas
ppeal: left to right, Margery Newton and Lynn Camsell of
ythe Bates Miners' Wives Support Group, Northumberland;
d Anne O'Donnell and Sue Davison of Bentley Miners'
ives Support Group, Yorkshire. *Sheila Gray/Format*

LOW LEFT A Meeting of Oakdale Women Against Pit Closures
Gwent, South Wales, in June 1984. *Jenny Matthews/Format*

Mary Hallum, age 60, who helped organise and run a 'soup' kitchen for eleven months in Edwinstowe, near Worksop in North Nottinghamshire. *Brenda Prince/Format*

proper heating for their homes! Of course their wives want to go to hairdresser! Of course they want a fortnight in the sun every year with their children!

But women living in the Rhondda think that the increase in living standards achieved in the 1970s will never be repeated – and they are almost certainly right. There is nothing for them now but the prospect of the dole.

The proof as they see it is in what happens to their children when they leave school. Although they have the same education as children in the rest of the country – they take O levels, A levels – they do not have the same opportunity as others to go to university if they get the required qualifications. As Rhondda parents know full well, it is still the children of rich parents who get opportunities for higher education, not children of working-class parents.

None of the women thought the mines were the way of life they wanted for their children when they were small. Mining had been a dirty, exhausting way of earning a living, with ill-health and early death through lung disease or injuries at the end of it. You will not find a miners' family that does not have secret hopes of something better for their children. The O levels and A levels, they used to think, were the way to this.

On the other hand, there was always the local pit for the boys if there were no other jobs. And many boys were eager to follow their fathers into the pits in a time of unemployment. The money was good. The developments of modern mining also seemed to offer new opportunities for bright kids as mining engineers or electricians.

Sandra, an organiser of the Maerdy Women's Support Group, explained how the old certainties had been shattered by the Tory government. Her son got seven 'marvellous' O levels. His parents thought he seemed set for university. But he wanted to work in the pits at a skilled job and to start work as soon as he could. He trained as a mining electrician, and qualified. But then he found he could not get a job.

With his seven O levels, he worked on a Youth Training Scheme. It was an unskilled job, with no prospects or hope of promotion. He left for work at seven in the morning and returned to his parents' home at seven at night, sometimes later if there was overtime, and usually exhausted. For this, he got £23 a week.

This is not an unusual story. Examples of exploitation, of low wages and long hours on Youth Training Schemes are repeated over and over again. One mother told of a 50-year old man being sacked to make way for a low-paid teenager and said it was common knowledge that this was happening all the time.

The miners and their families have always had an acute sense of politics when it comes to their working rights. During the strike that sense has greatly increased among the women.

Most of the women were trying for the first time to control their own destinies and their own lives. They were no longer simply a necessary extension of the miners and the pits.

There is no comparison between what the women are now and what they were at the beginning of the strike. Their mothers, they said, hardly recognised them and their grandmothers certainly would not have done so, even though some miners' wives had been imprisoned in 1926, and there is, in fact, a long record of women's support for miners' struggles.

There are grandmothers of women who ran the support groups in 1984 who retain clear memories of the strike in 1926. Then, heavy prison sentences were passed on hundreds of miners and their wives. In Swansea alone there were 395 cases of 'intimidation' heard during the lock-out.

'Red Mary' in the Rhondda had been famous during the 1926 employers' lock-out of the miners for the amount of coal she had managed to dig out of the 'drifts'– where coal had come to the surface – and had carried back to the villages each day.

The miners' wives in 1984, particularly in South Wales, were therefore following a long tradition of strength among the women. As in 1926 the imprisoned were welcomed when they came out, and helped – and not only by the mining community. (When nine men and two women came out of prison after serving sentences for their parts in a riot in 1926, a meeting was held for them at the Carmel Congregational chapel at Fochriw.

The minister presented the men with gold cigarette cases and the women with necklets and gold pendants, all of them inscribed.)

In 1926 some of the strikers and their wives followed the principle of refusing to pay fines and going to prison instead. In 1984–85 however, there was a general reluctance to choose imprisonment. The court system and operation of bail conditions were more sophisticated. Magistrates' courts sat until the early hours and dealt with cases quickly. That took the drama out of the situation. The opportunity for martyrdom was lessened. Even so, Greenham women on the miners' picket lines spent hours trying to persuade the miners and their wives to choose imprisonment rather than fines.

The leader of the Maerdy women's group did most of her work from a wheelchair. Babs Williams had been suffering from multiple sclerosis for the past few years. She had one son and a husband in the pits; even so, her courage remained undimmed at the end of the strike. 'Women are too well-organised, now, to let everything fall apart. We're going to build up this place; we're determined to. There's no cinema, no sports centre, nothing for the young ones. We're going to put that right, for a start!'

Babs said: 'There's going to be no more just being in the house and sitting on our backsides, now we know we can change anything if we are determined enough. We have really shaken the men. They thought we were content. But now they realise that we are not.'

Glynnis Evans had travelled through Britain and in Europe, speaking to raise funds for the miners. She had shared the same platforms with Tony Benn and Neil Kinnock. 'I was petrified, scared stiff about speaking at first. You have to be sure you can put your message across, but now I'm not scared. I'm prepared to travel anywhere.'

She could handle anything she wanted to, if she thought it was right and had set her mind to it. Yet before the strike she did not realise this. She was bound to the home, the children and the provision of meals at the end of a shift, her only relaxation being to watch the television, though not usually news documentaries.

Up to the start of the strike Glynnis's life had been circumscribed by the mining village. She says she knew little of the outside world. She offers a great deal of friendship to the world, but has no illusions about how the world regards miners.

The experiences of the strike had changed them all deeply. 'I'm less tolerant, for one thing,' said Glynnis, 'But I'm proud of myself now and what I have done during the strike.'

She says that there is not one family she knows in the Rhondda that has not been hit by tragedy at some time. Translate that into the context of any other job, and imagine all these workers living in one community, with most of them at some time being devastated by injury or illness because of it. This should give some indication of the closeness and solidarity of a pit community. There is a feeling that you have to stand together against the world outside.

'I'm not going to suffer like my mother did,' said Glynnis.

Her father died in a pit accident when she was small. Her mother was pregnant then. She had to be sent to live with her grandparents because her mother could not manage to look after her and the new baby at the same time.

She remembers clearly the day when the news came that there had been an accident with the winding machine at the pit, with her father the only casualty and the blow it dealt to her mother's life. 'And do you know how much they gave my mother? They gave her £100. That was what my father's life was worth.' Her father was only 29 years old.

Her mother eventually married again. But the story of disaster is now being repeated with her second husband. 'The dust has got at his lungs. It's terrible now to see him; he knows it is killing him.'

It was this knowledge that put fire into her speeches during the strike.

Glynnis was only one of many women in Maerdy who nerved themselves to do battle for their families. She did not regard herself as anyone special – she just happened to be the one who took me in for a cup of tea in her house on a dark, windy night in March and then sat with her husband, John, talking about the strike until the early hours.

The year of the strike was one in which Glynnis and John saw themselves as having developed intellectually, and with a new awareness of what was going on outside the valleys.

It was a remarkable story, and typical of the experience of many couples in the strike in pit villages all over Britain. Maerdy was twinned with Oxford. Oxford offered education and knowledge and an immediate grasp of the intellectual realities of why the miners were striking that was missing elsewhere. The Claimants' Union in Oxford started the twinning, but this rapidly expanded to other organisations. Maerdy people found themselves Oxford college guests, speaking from Oxford college platforms.

The Oxford support really started with a public meeting held at Ruskin college in May. A number of men and women from Maerdy were based there from Monday to Friday, going home only at the weekends.

John was in Oxford for much of the time, speaking, organising demonstrations and fund-raising. Then he would come home to the village to look after the children, while his wife went off to rallies and meetings. 'Women have done far more than men in the strike,' he said. 'They've done the administration, organised the meetings, the collecting and distributing of food, and they've been picketing, too.'

He would support his wife in almost everything she wants to undertake now – except going to Greenham. 'I respect the Greenham women, but don't want her to go there. I can't bear the thought of her being in danger.'

The most militant of Glynnis' children was the youngest, four-year-old Rebecca. She had been on many marches, and her clothes were covered with miners' stickers.

This seemed to be generally true of many mining families. It was the children under 12, particularly the girls, who threw themselves into supporting the strike, eager to go on as many marches as they could, collecting and exchanging badges and stickers. One nine-year-old girl had at least 100 badges all over her leather jacket.

Small girls became extremely knowledgeable about the NUM and about the pits. If you asked a girl's mother a question, the odds were that the answer would come from the daughter before the mother got a chance to say a word. Not only the miners' wives, but a whole generation of young women had been politicised.

There was an invitation for Maerdy children to go on holiday to France as guests. French unions were specially supportive during the strike. Did any children want to go? And an invitation for a speaker to go to Belgium. Any offers? Everyone was clearly used to this influx of invitations. The children had been all over the place on holiday, seeing foreign places for the first time and tasting foreign food. Just like their mothers, they would never be the same again.

Teenagers tended to keep their distance more. They were working for exams, or worrying about jobs. But they helped to keep households going. They had a better understanding of what their parents were going through and usually had the special burden of having to look after the younger ones and getting small jobs done around the home.

The number of pubs in the Rhondda has been cut from dozens to a few. But there are still places where you will find clusters of neighbours standing and talking outside their homes after midnight, on the way back from the pub and club as they used to do in the old days. It is a friendly habit that has died in most towns but still lives on in the Rhondda. There, night is not a time when doors shut against the outside world.

From the outside, the Working Men's Institute is an inimical looking building. In fact, the whole place looks blackened and deprived. Inside, however, it is very different. There is a feeling of friendship and warmth in the bar, where the miners and their families meet.

An example of this friendship is shown in the story of a brain-damaged boy who spends a lot of time in the club. He is intelligent and strong, but he cannot speak properly and he makes loud, embarrassing noises as a substitute for laughter. If he sits next to you, someone will be sure to come up and say that it is all right, that he is a good chap and not to be worried about him. He goes from table to table, talking to people. He communicates by writing notes. He fell off a wall playing football when he was ten, he explains, and was in a coma for a long time. Did he like it in Maerdy? 'After 21 years here, what can I say?' he wrote. All the people were like his own family.

It was clear that for the rest of his life he would be secure in the village. What would his future have been in London?

The boy's story really summed up the feeling of Maerdy's unitedness. But just as the village looked after its own, equally solidly it would turn on what it reckoned were its enemies. In this case not on scabs, for there were no scabs. (The miners told of one man who had been a scab in 1926. In all the time between the strike and his death no one had ever spoken to him. He had just died. People hated scabs more than they hated the government. They were the traitors in their midst, the ones taking the jobs away from them. They seemed to regard them as collaborators, as the Nazis in Europe were regarded during the Second World War. Scabs were the collaborators with the government and the bosses who were trying to take the jobs away.)

The enemies were MacGregor and the Tory government, epitomised by Mrs Thatcher.

The food distribution had started soon after the strike had begun. It had clearly been the NCB's hope that the miners' families would get so hungry that the women would be begging the men to go back to work. Instead, the Maerdy women started calling from door to door in the towns around asking for money for the miners' cause. By the third month, they were well organised. Over the Easter holidays they called a meeting and appointed their leaders. After that, the food parcel distribution started. They asked bakers, butchers and all the food shops for help. They were well received and had many donations. Even so, it was a hard, demanding job. The parcels had to be made up and then distributed. On a day when you had to distribute the food there would not be time or energy left for much else.

Maerdy Lodge was distributing 700 food parcels a week. The support group was also collecting and paying £600 a week to the NUM at Pontypridd. After a food-buying run to a cash and carry, £1,400 worth of food was delivered to Maerdy where it was divided into parcels. One of the committee said: 'We could only afford to put in the basics: eight pounds of potatoes, a tin of corned beef, a tin of veg, rice pudding, fruit, sometimes sugar, tea bags, tins of beans or spaghetti.' It was iron rations.

The working man's institute was where Babs Williams and her team brought the food they had collected to make it up into parcels for distribution. The parcels continued for about a week after the strike had ended and the support group itself continued until the people involved were sure that the families could manage on their own.

Kent

Few who are familiar with the orchards and the oast houses in Kent know where the pits are. They are comparatively new. But the threat of closure hung over them as surely as it did for pits in Scotland.

The miners came to Kent from all over Britain in the 1930s, with promises of work that would last them and their families well into the twenty-first century. Many had been union activists, sacked for their part in the 1926 strike. That was why they came.

The Kent miners are tough and determined. They probably inherit these characteristics from their fathers who walked to Kent from Scotland, Yorkshire, the north east and Wales to their new jobs.

There is a solidarity to be found within the Kent communities which cannot be found anywhere else – and also an instinct for survival. Kent miners were the last to go back at the end of the strike. Before they did, they went on one last picket up to

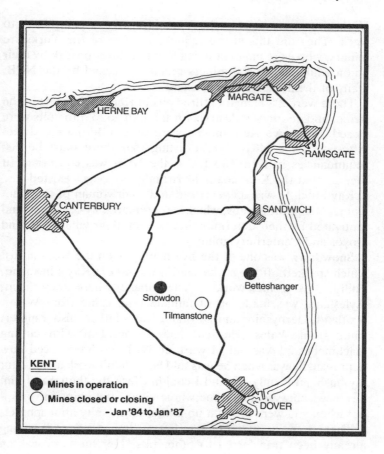

KENT

● Mines in operation
○ Mines closed or closing
 – Jan '84 to Jan '87

Yorkshire to try to stop the Yorkshire miners going back to work. They did this at the request of some of the Yorkshire miners, who were angry at being told to return to work by their union while nearly 800 miners remained sacked by the NCB, many of them local union officials.

There were 2,800 men in three pits in Kent at the start of the strike, and no other industries for them to go to if the pits were closed. Forty-two Kent miners were sacked during the strike. Afterwards the NCB were insisting that there must be 800 redundancies in Kent. So far as the NCB was concerned, it seemed that the Kent coalfield virtually no longer existed.

Kay Sutcliffe was 35 years old and chairwoman of the Kent women's support groups, which were remarkably organised and motivated by their determination to keep their villages around Dover and Canterbury going.

Snowdown was one of the five main pits on the NCB hit list which sparked off the strike, and it was where Kay's husband, Philip, was a face-worker. The village where they lived, Aylesham, was made up of families who came from Wales, Scotland, Derbyshire and Durham. Kay's father, also a miner, came from Wales. He had had an accident with cutting machinery and was out of work at 59. Kay remembered how depressed he was when he was told he couldn't work again. 'But my husband is only 36, and I couldn't face the thought of him never working again and the whole village not being in work – not when you were brought up in this community atmosphere.'

There were only 280 miners left at Snowdown, 200 having already been transferred to other pits. Her husband was an NUM branch official; his father a Yorkshire miner who still had a northern accent.

Kay has three daughters aged 15, 14 and 10 and used to work full time as an accounts clerk. Her thin frame seems to be burning with vision and energy. She started a women's group in 1972 and 1974.

It was mostly for food parcels and raising funds. But in 1974 there was no general aim, no understanding of what was going on in the rest of the country.

This time we called a public meeting straight away – and 40 women turned up. Then we organised a march to Coalville in the Midlands which, though it is so far away, is part of our area. Ninety women came on that march.

There were over 100 women in the support group and they ran a soup kitchen from Monday to Friday. Kay travelled, and both spoke and raised funds.

In October 1984 she was invited to West Germany to meet peace and environment groups and to speak about the strike.

The main job of the women's groups in Kent was to see that the children were fed. This they managed to do so successfully that when the strike ended and the kitchens closed the children were in tears when they had to go back to having their dinners at school. 'They'd been getting a good three-course meal in the kitchens every day, and they liked the atmosphere. Some children were really sobbing and not wanting to leave the kitchen, because they knew the friendships they had made would be gone when the men went back to work.'

We got an awful lot of help. What we experienced over 12 months has given everyone a much stronger feeling about what they can do against this government, which is trying to hit at the working class and break its spirit. We had to open the eyes of people who didn't understand what was going on. The tactics used not only against men on the picket lines but women as well showed that the government were prepared to do anything and use any amount of money to smash the NUM.

From the tactics the police used we have learned about violence and experienced it at first hand. It changed our attitudes and changed our children's attitudes. We no longer tell them to trust the police. The working-class struggle must go on now. What we've learned through violence is new to us, but it's been happening in Northern Ireland, in Liverpool, and to all minority groups – to blacks, gays, lesbians. These people were the first to come out on the picket line. It is a shame we never offered support before, but we'll fight every step of the way with them from now on.

6.
The Eye of the Storm

Nottingham's chequered support for militant action goes back a long way.

Before nationalisation, the coal-owners had always had relatively tame unions in Nottinghamshire. 'Spencerism' was a phrase revived in the 1984–85 strike, and it came from the aftermath of the 1926 lock-out in the pits. At that time the coal-owners had set up the Nottinghamshire and District Miners' Industrial Union, with the support of a Nottinghamshire miners' leader named George Spencer.

The Spencer movement dated back to attempts to form a non-political trade union movement early in the century. George Spencer became General Secretary of the Nottinghamshire Miners' Association and was a Labour MP. In the year of the general strike in 1926, he made a separate deal to get his members back to work on better terms than men in other areas.

The Spencer union in the Nottinghamshire area grew steadily during the 1920s and 1930s and the leaders of the Association wanted to expel Spencer. Continuous wage agreements with no strike deals were a particular feature. Spencer managed to keep wages relatively high even as he fought for a district union based on anti-Communism and a belief in market policy. It is easy to see why he was regarded as the predecessor to Roy Lynk, the leader of the working miners during the 1984–85 strike, though there were important differences between the two men in the way they operated.

The formation of the Union of Democratic Mineworkers was the outcome of a period of bitter inter-union struggle in the early months of the 1984–85 strike, which centred on Arthur Scargill's leadership.

Three areas voted in October 1984 to merge to form the new union – South Derbyshire, Leicestershire and Nottinghamshire – and Nottinghamshire got a 72 per cent majority in a 90 per cent poll. Roy Lynk was the new union's leader, and the ex-NUM official became the UDM's general secretary. The union was against Scargill; it has since weakened to the point of almost disappearing. During the strike, however, it represented the majority of the miners in Nottinghamshire who wanted to go back to work, thus following the county's right-wing history and its lack of the historical radicalism and solidarity of the Welsh, Scottish and Yorkshire coalfields.

The striking miners could not forgive the fact that Lynk was not expelled from the NUM during the strike. He was particularly hated by the Nottinghamshire strikers and the support groups, and his acceptance by the NUM – however unwilling – seemed to be a betrayal of their struggle.

Isolation

The wives of the miners striking in the Nottinghamshire coalfield were isolated from the rest of the women's support groups because over 27,000 Nottinghamshire miners had continued to work during the strike – the vast majority, in the county.

'At first Nottinghamshire didn't know whether they were on strike or whether they were at work. The ratio is about 8 to 1 against the strikers', said one woman, and another:

'It makes me angry because they're always on about how violent all strikers are supposed to be. But even if we wanted to be we couldn't, because we are in a minority. I mean, there's just us few.' (The strike ballot had shown a vote of 20,188 to 7,285 against striking.)

The women and their families suffered because of this isolation. In areas where the strike was solid, it had not been too difficult for women to find premises from which to run canteens and soup kitchens. In some pit villages in the north of England and Scotland, the pit villages were virtually organised from the miners' welfare halls. They were the source of all social life, providing treats and outings for the children and acting as advice centres for problems. Often these centres had behind-the-scenes backing from sympathisers in the local authorities.

This, however, was not the case in Nottinghamshire. Women had to occupy welfare centres in order to start up soup kitchens. Even so, as one woman said:

Our isolation made us come together very quickly.

Such a comment from Nottinghamshire women gives some idea of their feelings of isolation. But at Blidworth, Rainworth, Hucknall, Calverton, Ollerton and Clipstone, and all the pit villages where strikers were living, they got together, met each other on picket lines and began the support groups. The Strike Committees were formed, together with the Central Women's Support Group, to co-ordinate all the support groups. The Central Group had meetings twice a week, and each colliery support group sent its delegate. If one group seemed to be getting into difficulties, the others would help out.

The Clipstone Soup Kitchen

At Clipstone colliery the women stayed six nights in a youth centre owned by the National Coal Board, administered by trustees, and refused to leave. Finally the trustees agreed to give them premises where they could make and serve meals for the strikers and their families.

Occupation of a building is a pretty miserable business for those engaged in it. You are as much cut off from the world outside as prisoners – and that is totally. Usually the telephone is cut off. The police mount guard outside. It means going without any of the normal comforts such as meals, beds, or warmth, and on top of that there are worries about children and relatives.

It shows the determination of these Nottinghamshire women, and of how firmly they were behind the decision not to go back to work, that they stayed in the centre for a whole week to get what they wanted.

Many women were involved in the operation at Clipstone, among them Elsie Lowe, Margaret Anderson, Nellie Moore, Isabel Duncan, Claudia Jefferies, Jane Holness, Carole Potter and Barbara Neale. Elsie Lowe, the wife of John Lowe, the picket manager at Clipstone, was the leader of the group. She said:

> The occupation was well planned. When we started the soup kitchen we had no money, no food, and we were completely bankrupt. We had to find somewhere to run a kitchen, but we knew the NCB would stop us. We were being kept out of the youth centre so that we couldn't start anything, because they knew we were planning something.

They had tried asking the NCB for premises but had been refused. So one woman got her daughter to go into the youth centre on the grounds that she had left her watch in there. 'We all filed in after her quickly before they could stop us, and then barricaded ourselves in.'

After that they needed some food to keep going. They needed bread and onions to make soup.

By this time the police had put a guard round the centre. It was the police who went to the shop to get onions and brought them back without even asking for money in advance. Such police were of the kind who had little publicity in the strike, though many did exist, trained to help people where they could and to bring peace instead of violence to a community. The women made their police guard cups of tea – 'But we charged them for it.' Later, when the women themselves went to the shop for food, the police gave them protection and saw them in and out of the building. This was an incident that did not get reported, but there were many such, mingling together with the bloody pattern of the strike.

Finally, the trustees of the youth centre had a meeting and decided against eviction. They then met with the women and came to an agreement. They had to move out and instead were to be allowed to take over the local St John's Ambulance station building for the duration of the strike.

There had previously been a massive rally in Mansfield which had brought support for the strikers from all over the country and, for the support groups in Nottinghamshire, it provided a morale booster at a critical time. Elsie Lowe said:

People were getting hungry. There were getting on for 1,000 people we knew about who literally hadn't anything to eat. Soon they would be suffering from malnutrition. We knew we had to do something. We did it from the funds we raised ourselves. All the NUM money was going on keeping the pickets going.

The St John's Ambulance centre sounded a good idea, but when the women actually saw it they were downcast. There was only one cooker to cook for 1,000 people – and it was old and very dirty. 'The first thing we did was to clean that cooker,' said Elsie.

Once they had their own centre, the strikers, in isolated groups scattered around the villages and surrounded by the houses of working miners, began to cheer up. 'The centre kept our spirits up and the men and women got on all right together. The men made their own breakfast after picketing every morning at 5 am. It was a very long day if you were doing the cooking and serving. Most of the women got involved in it, even though many of them lived half an hour's journey away.'

John Lowe chipped in: 'The women organised the feeding well, right from the start. Once they got the premises – bang –

they were there! My admiration for them knows no bounds – the way they took over the organisation and catering and big-time buying without having had any experience of it before. It just seemed to happen. I'd no idea they could organise like that.'

Many of the women were still doing part-time jobs, as well, and others gave up jobs in order to work full-time in the soup kitchen.

They started off with one vanload of food from Cortonwood colliery in Yorkshire, where the strike had started. An article in the *Guardian* about Clipstone had brought in money from the Labour Party in London. They also got money from workers at the Greater London Council, British Telecom and from Pendle Labour Party, Pendle being Clipstone's 'twin' for the duration of the strike.

Blidworth Colliery

The surrounding villages totally depended on their pit, Blidworth. And other industries relied on the pit – which had come under review for closure by the NCB in 1983.

Blidworth had been working at a loss. But two new faces had been opened which would give coal for 50 years. If the strike was lost, though, the miners reckoned the first pit in Nottinghamshire to go would be Blidworth, because it had been designated as uneconomic. Hasty and ill-conceived top management decisions had ensured the pit was non-viable financially. It took the NCB about 15 months to open the two new faces, they said, whereas it should have taken only four months to do so.

There was a good case for keeping Blidworth open. It was known to have the best quality coal in the county, and it was mixed with coal from other pits to make it sell better. One woman said:

We feel so strongly about it. Why should they close Blidworth when there's all that coal to be got still, and all that money spent on it already? It would cost Maggie Thatcher a lot more to close the pit than it would to keep it open for 15 years. And I've got three teenage sons who could have a job at that pit for the next 50 years. None of them are working there at the moment, because their dad's on strike. If their dad had been scabbing, they'd have set them on. But there's jobs for my three lads there, if we win this strike. That's what it's about, really.

'We women have done it on our own, all through,' said one woman from Blidworth. 'We had to get somewhere to feed the kids because we knew that it was going to take a lot of money to give everybody food parcels, whereas if we got a kitchen we could feed people a lot cheaper. We decided to ask for the youth club to be lent to us. Well, we couldn't get it.'

NCB Propaganda

Striking miners had received letters saying that if they went back to work, their sons could have jobs, too. It was blackmail.

As the strike went on, it seemed to journalists that the NCB was prepared to offer any inducement to raise the scorecard of men going back to work. Moral and psychological blows were aimed at the strikers, and the NCB provided good propaganda with daily figures showing increases in the back-to-work figures. Most journalists did not believe them – they often did not tally with their own count of men going in and out – and they became something of a sour joke.

One woman said of the NCB figures:

I've seen one of those letters trying to get the men to go back. There's one youngish man going back to work at Shirebrook colliery, and he's been convicted of assaulting police and breaking windows on coal board property. He's completely wrecked a mechanical digger belonging to the NCB, yet he was told 'come back tomorrow morning and you can have your job back.' It's for the figures, you see. It's for the propaganda. They'll do anything to get them back.'

Violence and the Police

The surprise was that there was so little violent confrontation between strikers and workers. They were, after all, living next door to each other.

Linda King, at Ollerton, lived among working miners, but did not let that worry her. 'We can hold our heads up high; they can't – they daren't look you in the eye,' she said. But she was tolerant of what she regarded as their human weakness. 'They are green; they only think about what they get on a Friday. They can't see we are fighting for *their* jobs as well as ours.'

She had not felt isolated, she said. 'I've kept the friends I had before the strike, if their husbands were on strike, but those friends whose husbands carried on working, I don't want to bother with them any more, I really don't. I've nothing in common with them.'

The women used to take in the Yorkshire pickets in the soup kitchen and feed them. But it brought trouble for them.

When the police found out they were there they laid siege to the soup kitchen. They had house to house searches for the pickets and they broke into the soup kitchen. We were terrified.

The women blamed the police more than the scabs for the conflict. 'All I can say is, they're bastards,' said Linda King:

It was the police that caused the trouble between the strikers and the scabs. The police went out looking for trouble. They even knocked the women about for nothing. One morning in June we were in the welfare and the women decided to go with the men on the morning picket. We walked down the main street and the police tried to stop us. We were being quiet, because it was early morning and there were people with little 'uns in bed. The police told us to come over the road, and we said 'no', we were doing no harm.

'In Nottinghamshire, it's the strikers who are in the minority, so they are the ones who suffer. Subtle intimidation from the scabs, and not so subtle from the police,' said one woman. And another:

We tend to get attacked in pubs and then, by the time the police have finished with us, it's our husbands that always turn out to have done the attacking and they're the ones in trouble. The children get a lot of hassle from the others. They get called names for going to the soup kitchen. The others form a ring round the children going to the soup kitchen and just generally bully them . . .

One got me [said Linda King] and just banged my head up against the wall, just banged my head for nothing. This other one shoved me, so I went up to him and shoved him [she was a big woman] and then we just went back to the kitchen and had breakfast and went home. The look in that policeman's eyes when he banged my head – if there had only been me and him, he'd have given me some fist, but there were lots of men and women there. After that I was on my guard.

Her daughter, Rachel, nine years old and with a jacket covered with pickets' badges from all over Britain, went with her mother on some pickets at Ollerton. 'I'm glad I went. The men needed us,' she said.

Once Linda had to call an ambulance for a man taken by police on the picket line. 'They got this bloke and dragged him, and his leg got twisted and he was screaming out so I realised he was hurt. I shouted "Let him go" and got the ambulance and they took him to hospital. They kicked him; we saw that. We shouted, but there were that many police, no one heeded us.'

She was one of the people who found herself nearly arrested

for being visible in her own village. 'It was later that day, and I was sitting on a little wall. The police asked me to move and I said "I'm not doing anything, I'm just sat here. If this was an ordinary day, you wouldn't give a damn".'

So they fetched a superior officer who told her that unless she moved from her wall she would be arrested. In the end she did, because Rachel was at school and would want her tea later. 'I wouldn't let them escort me and the pickets started cheering and waving.'

There was no end to the arrests, but the ever present threat of being arrested had not stopped people from going out at night. 'We still went to the chippy, and went to meet each other. If the men had stopped going out, it would have looked as though the police had beaten us.'

Others were not so robust. One woman from Blidworth said just before Christmas 1984: 'The police were outside the house day and night in summer and we're still suffering from that, even now. They've never left us alone. The amount of money the government have spent on the strike would have kept every pit open for 25 years. It's not just a case of closing pits; it's a case of smashing the NUM. This is what it's all about.'

'But Margaret Thatcher made the big mistake of underestimating the women in this strike,' said a friend of hers. As she said this, they were waiting outside a courtroom in Nottingham for friends brought up on minor charges connected with picketing. 'She thought we'd send the men back to work because we've got a mortgage and want a holiday. But that's not what is important.'

Another woman said bitterly: 'This is something that has been planned for the last 10 years, ever since we won the strikes in the 1970s. Buy your houses, get your hire purchase and your Visa cards, and then we'll have a go at you, they thought. It's the same with the police. The police have been trained these last 10 years to do the job they're doing, and now I'm afraid we are never going to get rid of the policing we've had in the strike.'

Then the Nottinghamshire villages themselves came under

siege. The police cars cruised day and night around the streets, pouncing on pickets whenever they found them, going into houses to arrest them. The families lived under virtual curfew. Just stepping outside the front gate might lead to arrest – and often did. A man would go out to the 'chippy' and fail to return. It would only be late the following day that his wife would find out that he was at the local police station.

The ease with which a virtual police state could take over if people went against authority frightened the people of Nottinghamshire. If this could happen during a miners' strike, might it not just às easily and as quickly happen in some other situation where people were opposing government policy?

People did accept that if a criminal offence were to be committed, such as assault on a working miner, or robbery, then criminal law would have to be used against the criminal. But people were being arrested for nothing, just for existing. Men were being arrested just because they were not at work in Clipstone colliery, as the NCB said they should be.

During the strike it was impossible to move freely in areas where you might be suspected of being a sympathiser with the strikers. You felt you had to dodge the police in case of arrest. Presumably this was one reason why most journalists stayed safely on the right side of the police and did not investigate the cries of protest about civil injustice that were pouring out of Nottingham. In fact, the magistrates' courts had to sit until three in the morning to deal with all the people being brought in front of them.

John Lowe was arrested while sitting on the grass outside his own pit, and refusing to move. 'I had six police on to me at once, yet I was charged with hitting two policemen and actual bodily harm. They had to drop the last charge.'

Family Divisions

One of the worst aspects of the conflict of loyalty in Nottinghamshire was the divisions within families. There were quarrels which, it seemed, would never be patched up. One woman who enjoyed the strike because of the new friends she had made, and the reserves of strength she had discovered in herself and her friends, suffered deeply when her son went back to work. 'The hardest thing for me was that. He went back in June. His dad then kicked him out.' She was not really able to talk about it – it went so deep. Her husband was a Welsh miner with strong Welsh traditions of solidarity, and had to come to Nottinghamshire for work in the 1960s.

> He wasn't really militant, but he's always said that if there is a picket on, you can't cross it. And our son did. I know why he went back; he did it for the money. The single lads got nothing from the social, nothing at all. He was living at home, but that meant that they took £16 off my money because he was there – that was the strike money he was supposed to be getting, though the social knew none of them were actually getting it. That left us £10 a week for four of us, plus the family allowance. So I couldn't give my son 'owt out of that.

> His father still does not speak to him. But she said, quickly and casually, that she kept in touch with him. He was all right. 'He's buying his own place now; he did the best thing from his point of view.' Her sister's husband had stayed on strike until December and then he, too, had gone back.

It was not only the high wages and modern pits as well as the comparative proximity to Birmingham and London and the non-mining worlds of material ease which caused the deep splits in Nottinghamshire. It was also the fact that people from the villages came from different mining backgrounds and had settled in the area without any common roots. They had not built up the solidarity to be found in Kent. Linda King, for example, said she was surprised by how many Scots had gone back to work in Nottinghamshire.

There was a lot of bitterness directed towards the striking miners from the scabs.

The scabs come out of the pit waving their wage packets at us and saying, 'Our kids will have a good Christmas, what about yours?' That sort of thing.

Most of the strikers' wives had members of their own families still working down the pit. 'Not all the families are split. It's mainly us big mining families that have been in the pits from generation to generation,' said one. 'It's amazing, really, because most of the people I know originally came from Yorkshire where they're strongest.'

One woman's father had crossed the picket lines, another had a brother who had refused to strike. 'My husband's family have completely cut us off and have said we all want sending to Russia,' was one woman's wry comment. She added sadly: 'They say we've been a great embarrassment. So that's it. We've lost a family. But we've gained a new family.'

Another woman supporter of the strikers said: 'My mother blames Arthur Scargill for losing her only daughter. I mean, it couldn't have been a very close relationship if Arthur Scargill has broken me and my mother in two! She had the gall to say to my daughter, who's expecting a baby, that when the baby is born and the strike's over, she will be coming to see them every Wednesday. Best of British luck, I say. I hope she gets fed the same as she's fed me the last 10 months – which is nothing.'

Another said: 'My daughter went into a shop the other day and there were two aunts in there. She said hello to them. They just didn't answer her. Just cut her completely dead as if she wasn't there – and that was to a child. It's their guilty consciences, because they know deep down they are wrong; they *know* they're wrong.'

Miners' Wives and Minority Groups

The wives of striking miners in Nottinghamshire had discovered minority groups. Before, they had always seen themselves as a working-class elite, and at first it was a shock to find that in police eyes they rated as blacks, teenagers with drugs, or gays.

It was a healthy awakening.

'We didn't realise what the minority groups were suffering – the blacks and the others,' said Doreen Humber.

I went to Brixton for a time and stayed there during the strike, speaking and fund-raising. I saw where the blacks had imprisoned the police in the police station during a riot. I'm not a person that likes violence, but I just thought, good, I'm glad they imprisoned them'. What we've been living through, they've had to live through for years, and it's spoiled their lives and their children's lives. We can't any longer sit back looking at television and say, 'Oh, isn't that terrible, but there's nothing I can do.' After this strike, we shall always help other people. We shan't stop fighting because we know now we can fight. We realise that other people have got struggles, too, and that their struggles are part of what we are fighting for. We've got to continue with this supporting of each other through *everything* they throw at us.

Under the title 'Women for Mines not Missiles' a joint demonstration was held in August 1984 of the Women Against Pit Closures groups and Women for Peace. They staged a four-day march from the Capenhurst nuclear processing plant to the Nottinghamshire coalfield to protest at the government's claim that pits had to close because of the lack of demand for energy and that, at the same time, this same government was planning to spend billions of pounds on building new nuclear power stations. In their regular bulletin, the Nottinghamshire Women's Support Groups had asked: 'Why is the government planning to build nuclear power stations?' The answer, they concluded, was simple. 'First they want to break the power of the mineworkers and railworkers. Second, nuclear power produces a waste product called plutonium. Plutonium is used to make warheads for nuclear missiles.'

Nottinghamshire Women and the Barnsley March

The march that the Women Against Pit Closures organised in Barnsley was huge. It drew 10,000 women from all over the country, rather than only the few hundred they were expecting. A group of women went from Nottinghamshire and the Barnsley women put them in an important position, right in the middle. Up until then, the Nottinghamshire women had been feeling rather guilty when they were asked where they came from. 'You had to explain yourself to the other miners; people seemed to think we were all scabs, they didn't realise how many were on strike in the county.'

In Yorkshire they suddenly found themselves heroines. It had been a sensitive psychological move on the part of the Yorkshire women to put them in the middle of the march, and it marked a turning point in Nottinghamshire. 'We went through Barnsley singing "Notts are here, Notts are here".

'We walked through Barnsley, singing, and it was fantastic. Everybody was cheering and shouting for us.'

The Barnsley group asked Doreen Humber to speak, even though she was not at all prepared to do that. 'I just stood up in front of those 10,000 people and said: "I'm speaking on behalf of Nottinghamshire." I didn't know what response we were going to get. But it was just great, people saying "You're fantastic, you're brilliant".'

Susan Petney added: 'At first it was odd, because they just didn't believe us. They thought we were all scabs in Notts, but they were great when they realised.'

A Fight for the Future

One woman said:

The last strikes were only for money. The women stayed at home then. We knew this time that it was a lot more than that. We realised it was a fight for our future. We knew this

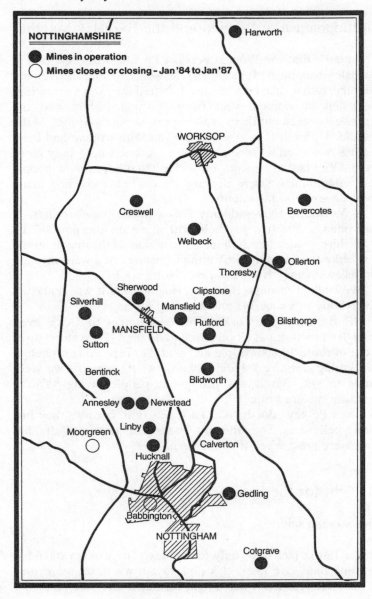

NOTTINGHAMSHIRE

● Mines in operation
○ Mines closed or closing – Jan '84 to Jan '87

Harworth

WORKSOP

Creswell

Bevercotes

Welbeck

Ollerton

Thoresby

Sherwood

Clipstone

Silverhill

Mansfield

MANSFIELD

Rufford

Bilsthorpe

Sutton

Bentinck

Blidworth

Annesley

Newstead

Moorgreen

Linby

Calverton

Hucknall

Gedling

Babbington

NOTTINGHAM

Cotgrave

wasn't going to be a strike settled over night, because though we weren't political before the strike, we could see what was happening to the country. Every time you switched on the news there were more industries closing down and more people getting on the dole. So we used to think: when it hits us what are we going to do? We knew the miners were going to be attacked, and when it finally hit us, we knew that it was going to be a long job – though not as long as this. Us women decided we had to feed the kids and sort something out. So what we did first off, we got leaflets printed, started speaking at Labour Party meetings, trade union council meetings, things like that, getting money together.

Now the Nottinghamshire women who supported the miners are in the midst of a greater struggle. More unemployment has come to the coalfields, just as they knew it would. Even though so many miners worked throughout the strike this has not safeguarded their jobs.

The women have both to support the sacked and unemployed miners, and to learn to live together once more with those they still call scabs. It is a matter for history whether they will ever be able to do this; on past experience, it would seem very doubtful.

7.
Changing Relationships

Women work as miners in the United States. On a recent tour of Britain the women quoted high wages well beyond the aspirations of most women workers in Britain. They also complained about bad conditions and male harassment. On the whole, though, they are proud of their work and their strength. America does not have Britain's sex barriers, and there are women road menders and truck drivers, in the United States, as in the Soviet Union.

In Britain, however, you will not find a miner's wife or an NUM woman member or anyone in the Women Against Pit Closures organisation who thinks that women should go back down the mines. There is a dark history in this country of women's labouring down the pits. Mining, like lighthouse-keeping, is one of the few jobs not protected by the modern equal opportunities legislation, which on paper gives women a right to compete fairly for any job.

Even in the nineteenth century employment of women and children down the pits varied from area to area. Not one woman was employed in the Derbyshire collieries, either above or below ground, until the First World War, when there was employment of women miners for the first time in this area.

The Derbyshire Miners' Association – the working miners – had taken the lead in demanding an amendment to the Coal Mines Bill of 1911, prohibiting the employment of all women on pit banks.

It was the women suffragists who helped to defeat the amendment, on the grounds that women wanted to do the surface work because they needed the wages. The suffragists were attacked by politicians and male pit workers alike. 'University women carry out an agitation and try to prove how nice and comfortable the work is, but they do not have to earn their livelihood on the pit bank,' said Robert Smillie, a miner's leader.

Another man said:

It is surprising to me that in this twentieth century, when training for home life is said to be so essential, that we should have factors at work from the cultured part of life trying to keep down the wives and daughters of the workers . . . I am proud to say . . . that there are counties in England and Wales where there is no such thing as women employed on the pit banks. We long ago believed that that was not the place for women. The place for women is the home, in order to make the home happy.

The introduction of women into the engine house, stores and lamp cabin at the Haleswood colliery in Derbyshire in 1916 caused consternation. The men were dismayed, because they wanted the women to stay in the home. During the war, one of the new women workers was put to doing work formerly carried out by a disabled man, who, in turn, was transferred to heavier work which proved too much for him. A strike was threatened – and the women were withdrawn.

Women and the NUM

The question of associate membership and the right of women to take part in strike consultations in the NUM was a burning issue after the strike for women activists and is a subject for debate within the NUM itself.

In June 1984, Jean McCrindle, the National Treasurer of the

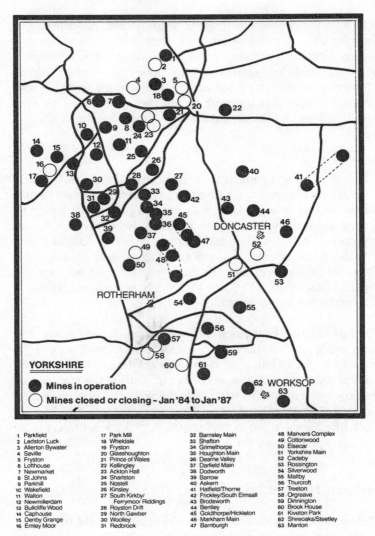

YORKSHIRE

● Mines in operation

○ Mines closed or closing – Jan '84 to Jan '87

1 Parkfield	17 Park Mill	32 Barnsley Main	48 Manvers Complex
2 Ledston Luck	18 Wheldale	33 Shafton	49 Cottonwood
3 Allerton Bywater	19 Fryston	34 Grimethorpe	50 Elsecar
4 Saville	20 Glasshoughton	35 Houghton Main	51 Yorkshire Main
5 Fryston	21 Prince of Wales	36 Dearne Valley	52 Cadeby
6 Lofthouse	22 Kellingley	37 Darfield Main	53 Rossington
7 Newmarket	23 Ackton Hall	38 Dodworth	54 Silverwood
8 St Johns	24 Sharlston	39 Barrow	55 Maltby
9 Parkhill	25 Nostell	40 Askern	56 Thurcroft
10 Wakefield	26 Kinsley	41 Hatfield/Thorne	57 Treeton
11 Walton	27 South Kirkby/	42 Frickley/South Elmsall	58 Orgreave
12 Newmillerdam	Ferrymoor Riddings	43 Brodsworth	59 Dinnington
13 Bullcliffe Wood	28 Royston Drift	44 Bentley	60 Brook House
14 Caphouse	29 North Gawber	45 Goldthorpe/Hickleton	61 Kiveton Park
15 Denby Grange	30 Woolley	46 Markham Main	62 Shireoaks/Steetley
16 Emley Moor	31 Redbrook	47 Barnburgh	63 Manton

Women Against Pit Closures in Sheffield wrote to the *Sunday Times* that an associate membership category within the NUM would be welcome to the new women's organisations which had grown up during the NUM's struggle to preserve jobs, communities and life in the north of England. 'These women's support groups overwhelmingly consist of the women members of miners' families desperately anxious about their futures. Associate membership of the NUM would preserve their connection with the union and would provide a forum for information and discussion between the union and the wider community.' But Yorkshire had already turned down the idea, and most of the NUM was against it.

Florence Anderson was a local county councillor in Durham. Her father had been a miner, a strong trade unionist, an NUM member and a socialist, but she is not at all sure what he would think about women being regarded on the same level as miners.

During the strike, in the north east, the men were careful to remain in charge. In Hetton during the strike, 'The orders just came from above. There were no joint meetings. They didn't say "We're doing this, we need your support." If they had anything on they wanted organised it was like the tablets of stone coming down. And that grieved us a wee bit, because we felt the men weren't regarding us as equals.'

Eventually the women almost commanded the men to come to their meetings, which in the end they did – reluctantly. But when they tried to go to a union meeting at the start of the strike they were told: 'You're not allowed in the union meeting. Stand by the door; we're not ready for you yet.'

The women had to sit on the stairs, waiting for the men to decide to give them permission to serve them in the soup kitchens. It was an ordeal when they were finally allowed in and had to walk down the hall in front of all the miners staring at them.

The women spoke to them, setting out what they wanted to do in the kitchens, and saying why they had wanted to have a joint meeting to start with, to make it easier for the project to be set up. The men were not exactly hostile. They asked questions. Where were the women going to get the pans from? What menus where they going to put on? But they didn't give their approval. They didn't give any sign that they recognised the value of what the women were offering to do. And there were never any joint meetings. The women were never able to discover what was going on in the NUM and they were told quite definitely that they could not go to union meetings.

'They told us we couldn't do this and we couldn't do that,' said one woman. 'And they'd say "How dare you interfere in our area! We don't want you in our area; you're all right in the kitchen".'

The women wanted to go picketing but most of the men were against it. After Christmas, when the going got rough, attitudes changed. But there was one NUM leader, admitting happily that he was the original male chauvinist pig, who deliberately got them a car to go picketing at four o'clock in the morning in six feet of snow. 'If you don't take this on, you're not going picketing any more. I'm not laying anything else on for you,' he said. The women suspected that the men might have been waiting to see if they would fall flat on their faces, and then they would have been able to say 'I told you so'.

By the time the strike ended, however, the men were appreciating almost everything the women were doing for them, said Florence Anderson.

Sometimes they even worked under the women's instructions. In the panic of Christmas preparations, and the toy and turkey appeal, the women in the Eppleton Area Miners' Wives' Support Group needed the miners' help. Florence produced a leaflet called 'Instructions for T Day' (Turkey Day). The miners took it very seriously. One of them kept putting on his glasses to check the instructions to make sure he was getting it right. Florence said she was touched.

When the strike was over and the kitchen had closed the men thought that that was the end of it all. But the working-class women had become thoroughly politicised by then. At first, most women had been ignorant about politics and committee procedure. After her first meeting in Hetton, Florence said that she practically reeled off the platform, because she had been used to council meetings and the women's meeting had been one of the most confused she had ever attended in her life. The outlook appeared to be gloomy. Gradually, however, the women learned and became practised at politics, just as the miners had in the past.

Breaking through the frustration were moments of sheer triumph. The National Union of Public Employees on Teeside wanted to organise playgroups for the children for the summer, and asked for young miners to take charge of them. 'I went into the welfare and said "Somebody wants some miners to look after the children during the summer," and there was uproar,' said Florence.

Everyone was trying to get out of it. One pointed out that he worked at a different pit and was not, strictly speaking, an Eppleton miner. But the NUPE women were determined. They argued the men into it. 'It was a tremendous sight to see the lads weighed down with kids and everything, doing the shopping while the women were working in the welfare centre. It was a real reversal of roles.'

The women had been determined to keep their support groups going after the strike. But it was not easy. Said Florence:

For working-class women, if your husband is on night shift, it isn't easy to get to meetings. My husband is working at tub loading, going to work at 6 at night until 12 midnight. It's not his fault, but I can't get out of the house now. I have to look after my daughter. Women have difficulty getting to support group meetings, specially those with small children. But the group is going on. We are determined to have a say in our own lives from now on.

Alan Cummings, the secretary of Easington colliery lodge, after the strike, took a more optimistic view than Florence Anderson of the new role the women might now have – though he had no doubt that they were going to have a difficult time. The strike, he thought, had probably changed men's attitude to the women.

> There's the image of the Geordie man with a cloth cap and a
> little woman at home. He drinks his beer and races his
> pigeons. But I don't think that image has been true for a long
> time, here. So far as the women are concerned, I think the
> real activists will carry on. But many may go back to how they
> were before the strike. It's over for them once the men are
> back at work.
>
> If my wife wants to go to a meeting, that's fair enough. I
> stay in. The men might grumble, but I think they are proud of
> the women. It's not women's lib as such, is it? We're all on
> about equality and that's what the women should have. I
> think men can recognise that the women's role has changed.
> My attitudes may be different to some of the older men, but
> my son's attitude is probably different to mine.

Alan Cummings belongs to the liberal group of NUM officials
who think the union should have associate membership for the
women. 'They did more than make tea and biscuits. It would be
a sign of recognition.'

At the Colliery Inn, near the Murton colliery in Durham,
which is part of the same group of pits as Easington, Mary
Parry, of the Murton Wives' Support Group, said of the miners'
attitudes: 'We've even had union men turn to us, saying, "The
strike's finished, what are you still doing around here now?"
One said to us, "I thought I'd seen the last of you".'

Another woman who had helped to keep the strike going for
the miners said that one husband she knew had said that he'd
'wanted his old wife back'. It was painful, she said. If it hadn't
been for the women the strike wouldn't have lasted as long as it
did.

One woman said there was a miner nearby who thought
women were rubbish and should never have been allowed to get
involved in the strike in the first place.

Heather Wood, of the Save Easington Area Mines Group,
and also a county councillor from a mining family and married

to a miner, commented rather sadly that 'During the strike the women were built up by the men. They thought the union was still going to pay the same attention to them after the strike.' They were wrong.

The Easington Group used the organisation they had built up to improve not only their lives but other people's lives after the strike had finished. The women carried on with their public speaking. There was a campaign to save a local maternity hospital, to help the sacked miners and their families, and many women who before the strike had not been interested in politics joined the Labour Party.

But sometimes, Heather confessed, she got fed up and couldn't see them winning through. 'We gave our all last year. You get depressed the way things are going. The worst thing of all is that the prime minister should be a woman.'

The fact that the women have become more politicised has scared the local NUM, thought Florence Anderson. 'I love the NUM dearly, I love their traditions, I love the banners, I love everything about them, but they really are the bastion of male chauvinism. To a certain extent I think they are afraid of the women – they were afraid of them in the strike, and they are still afraid of them.'

There was a revealing conversation at the end of a party after the strike, when tongues were free in the early hours. 'You got certain members of the NUM – we won't mention their names – saying "I've never liked you, you'll never dominate us". They said, "We'll demolish you if you start trying to dominate us," and "You'll never get into our union".'

The women noticed that they themselves had been quicker at starting things, getting things done, having ideas, and putting them into practice. That was what had frightened the men. The men were slower and more conservative, not so inspired. That is why they might have been frightened of letting the women anywhere near their union.

The information coming to the women from the union meetings, therefore, was second-hand, mostly via their husbands. This was frustrating for the support groups. For instance, the women wanted to get buses to bring the men who lived far away to the strike centre, and to send them leaflets, but the union was against it. 'Our support organisation would have been different if we'd been really in charge of it; it would have been more streamlined,' said one of the women. 'We would have made an effort to go out to the members and keep them informed. One woman was very upset because she lived outside the Hetton area and had phoned a lodge official asking for advice. He had put the phone down on her. She had three children and both she and her husband were loyal to the union, but they'd received no help. Just talking to her, making arrangements to get her children up to the Christmas party – it satisfied her that somebody cared about her.'

The officials were too busy with other things to talk to miners' wives and calm them down. The women could understand that. But they themselves did have time and were prepared to sit and listen to people. So why didn't the NUM accept that and let the women get on with organising things the way they wanted to, instead of resenting them and putting a stop to their activities?

For women members of the NUM non-involvement in union activities was sometimes caused by an inability to stand up to the pressures. Alfreda Williamson, an 18-year-old canteen worker and NUM member, confessed that she hadn't even gone to the meeting held to decide on the return to work. 'I just waited till someone came out and explained what the meeting had to say. I still wouldn't go now, not on my own with 50 or 100 men there.'

How would a male trade unionist feel if the situation were reversed?

Alfreda had been an activist in the strike. The picketing had been harder for her than it had for the men. She got £2 a day picket money, the only income she had. At 4 o'clock in the morning she went to make the tea in the welfare hall before she went up to join the picket at the pit gates at Murton. Afterwards, she went back to the welfare hall to make tea for the other pickets. 'Then we had all the washing up to do before we were finished, so we were working a lot harder than the men, and I told a few of them that and all, when they used to come and complain.' She tried to get out of making the tea and to go out in the buses with the other pickets, but the union wouldn't agree to this.

The women did not think they had been treated properly as NUM members. It really is not surprising that women in general are regarded as poor trade unionists. The unions are male dominated, with few exceptions, and women's rights are not regarded as a serious part of any conference agenda. If a woman worker, particularly if she has children, does not look out for herself, there is no one else to look out for her.

If she loses her job, or her wages are too low or her hours are too long, she can expect precious little help from male trade unionists, as the history of women's strikes demonstrates. Other women might help her, but men won't – unless they have a special reason for doing so. So why should women be enthusiastic about men's strikes? The really remarkable thing about the miners' strike was that this time the women *were* on the men's side.

Alfreda and her friends tried to prevent other NUM canteen women going in to work by stopping them and talking to them. When a vote was taken on a 50p levy off wages to help the sacked miners, Alfreda went to vote for it. The man sitting by the voting box looked on his list and told her she wasn't there and couldn't vote. 'I says, I pay my union money every week, I've got a right to vote, but he just said I hadn't. The union secretary came over and I said to him, "Look, I pay my union money every week, why can't I vote?" We got our vote in the end, and we should be able to vote on everything without all that.'

It was not surprising, Alfreda thought, that two women had gone back to work – in the canteens and offices at the pits – during the strike. 'The thing that had maddened them was that whenever they went to the union for help, they weren't interested in their case. When they went to complain about things that were wrong, they just said they'd let them know next week, but they never did. In their own minds, the ones who went back did so because the unions never bothered about them.' In a way, it was quite surprising that only two had gone back to work, she thought, considering how they had been treated.

Alfreda said: 'We work eight-and-a-half hours a day, longer than the men, and we don't get the same breaks as them. And if the dinners are late – the noise they make!'

One woman said that after the strike the union had done bugger all for the families and the sacked miners. 'It's been left to the women.'

Philip Bell, a young miner at Murton and son of the lodge treasurer, told Alfreda that when the younger men took over in the future, things would get better for the women. She, however, was not convinced.

There were also problems with the Welsh NUM. As in other areas, the NUM often seemed to take notice of the women's support groups when they thought they could be useful – and at other times ignored them. After a big women's picket at Port Talbot, however, the women's courage and worth were proved. Some of the NUM suggested they occupy Cwm colliery. A women's picket was organised, only to discover that the pit lodge itself knew nothing of the idea. So the women asked to see a plan of the pit, where the police would be stationed, and where the workings were. They said if they had carried out the occupation as asked by the NUM they would have negotiated a difficult climb down a bank at the pithead only to rush straight into the arms of the police. They turned down the idea. Even so, the women said that some members of the local NUM executive refused to have anything to do with them after that.

Cwm colliery has since closed (November 1986).

The miners' national leaders, in particular Arthur Scargill, wanted to introduce associate membership for the women in the support groups. It would mean a change in the NUM rules, but he did not see that as a problem. It would confer no rights or privileges or voting status, and certainly offer little chance to attend union meetings, but it would give the women's support groups due status. Also, associate membership would be like a medal for the women's work during the strike.

Yorkshire, Scargill's own area, proceeded to turn the idea down flat. 'They'll be wanting a seat on the Executive next,' said one of those who voted against.

'They hoped we'd just toddle back to the kitchen,' said one of the Barnsley Women Against Pit Closures committee.

Wales, too, rejected the idea. Welshmen are said to have a special empathy with women and women gave them the credit for seeing that associate membership might only tie them down more firmly to traditional male structures – something they did not want.

Scotland, on the other hand, led by the NUM vice-president Mick McGahey, just went ahead and made the women in its support groups associate members of the NUM, without fuss or publicity. The women took their place at union and party conferences.

It is inevitable that women will be made associate members when space is again found for the matter on the NUM conference agenda. At such a time in the future it may not matter so much as it did at the annual conference after the strike in July 1985. That conference concentrated on the presence of the representatives of the controversial Nottingham working miners. As usual women were pushed off the agenda. It was a repetition of the way things used to happen – women's rights went firmly to the end of the queue, to be dealt with only after 'more urgent' things had been set right. The miners at the conference threw out the resolution on associate membership, while the women who had helped them throughout the strike demonstrated angrily outside. Now they were no longer so necessary they were were outsiders again. It was a wounding snub, and a repetition of the way women had been treated, for example, after two world wars. The message was being spelt out loudly and clearly that they should get back to the kitchen.

Nevertheless, in spite of the family problems and quarrels this issue has caused, they have not done so.

The miners can recognise an injustice when they see it, for

they have suffered plenty of it themselves. Will they be able to admit that they have exploited women as they have themselves been exploited?

The Eppleton Area Miners' Wives' Support Group

Durham had a reputation for militancy during the strike. The rundown of its coalfield has been relentless. In the 1950s, Durham employed over 100,000 men in 114 pits. At the end of the strike there were only 13 pits.

The villagers of Hetton-le-Hole regard themselves as living in County Durham, though officially they live a few miles north of the border, in Tyne and Wear. Hetton is home for many miners at Eppleton pit in the Durham coalfield.

At Hetton, the men were astounded, and are still scratching their heads, about how much the women managed to take on during the strike. They had not realised how strong they were.

The women had a punishing routine. Having prepared the pickets' breakfasts, they would immediately start on the dinners. The food parcels' staff would work with men on the food parcels. Long before all this they would have been up in the early hours of the morning on the picket line. They reckoned they had worked physically harder than men. On the other hand, the men were getting battered on the picket line, and this did not happen to the women, said one of the Eppleton wives. She added that some of the men did help to wash up in the soup kitchen.

In the kitchens, the conditions had been extremely primitive. At Eppleton, there was only one cooker to make 200 meals a day. And there were also the pickets' breakfasts in the morning. Two women were badly scalded in the kitchen because of the conditions.

Florence Anderson has a peaceful recollection of the summer of 1984.

What a glorious summer it was! That's what you remember

about the strike. The atmosphere was great. If you can say you enjoyed the strike, in the summer we did. It was beautiful. There was a journalist who came up from Newcastle to speak to us, to do an article about us. We took her up to Eppleton – you go up the winding country lane on to the hill. The pickets were sitting up there, sunbathing. It was just a token picket. They had their little wee hut up there and they seemed to be up in the hills away from everything. It was lovely up there, peaceful and quiet.

But when the first scab went in the first week of November, everything changed. The weather was changing too, then, and the mass pickets started at Eppleton. The scab didn't belong in Hetton, he was an outsider. He wasn't one of us. That was the pattern, of course. He'd probably been worked on by the National Coal Board who were trying to break the strike. Well, the women went to the pit to picket every day after that.

The men didn't ask us to go picketing; we decided ourselves. We went up at about 7 o'clock. We met the first set of police across the roadway up to the pit and they really looked horrible. They had this scowl about them. The police dogs were at their side and one man was standing wearing jodhpurs with his hands on his hips. The lads said 'They won't let you through, don't try it,' but we marched on and the police just opened up and let us through and then we walked further on and there was another set of police but they moved aside and we went and stood with the men and the men cheered and applauded us that morning.

They were pleased by the men's attitude. 'OK, we'd worked in the kitchen and we had a good relationship with the men, feeding them and their families. But we weren't sure about picketing, because the men had never really encouraged us. They were frightened we'd be harassed by the police and hurt.'

On one occasion, after distributing leaflets and being removed physically and bruised by the police, Florence spent two hours trying to submit an official complaint to an inspector.

He tried to talk her out of it.

> He said that I ought to be ashamed of the mob outside (it was actually our women singing) and that we were the cancer in society. He said Margaret Thatcher was the best leader this country had ever had and what he thought ought to happen to Arthur Scargill was nobody's business. I had to listen to all this political tirade.

She complained again when her daughter received a threatening phone call. The same inspector came to see her.

> He sat for about three hours and we had to go through all his politics again. What he thought about the miners – the miners were thugs, and if he ever saw my husband on the picket line, he'd beat him. I couldn't believe what I was hearing. I said I've never heard such extreme views in all my life. I said: 'You're Alf Garnett in uniform.' He said that the Labour councillors were all Marxist–Leninists. There was a young lassie from our group there at the time so I says to her, 'Are you a Marxist–Leninist man?' She said she didn't understand what I was talking about.

It seems unlikely the inspector would have talked like that to a man. Many Durham men seem to have a peculiarly patronising attitude to women. 'We're going to have trouble with these women, once the strike's over,' said one pit delegate to a visiting SOGAT official from London.

Eppleton merged with Murton Colliery in September 1986.

Walking Wounded

The strike has produced plays, literature, songs and pictures from the mining communities, particularly from the women.

The mining communities produced their own record of the events of the strike, and nothing can match the vivid local immediacy of those accounts. One of the best was *Strike 84–85* a booklet produced by the North Yorkshire Women Against Pit Closures. In the foreword there was a quotation which read as follows:

> In the coalfields, there is a new breed of women who are only as old as the strike, who have won the admiration of people the world over. They have fought not behind their men but shoulder to shoulder with them. When histories of the strike are written, all will agree that the women were glorious.

In the accounts of their role in the strike, some women reveal that before the strike they were the walking wounded of the male mining world. And these were the same women who were willing to exist on £11.95 a week for themselves, two children and a husband. It was their basic DHSS allowance and it kept the strike going.

One woman wrote:

> I've had a rough marriage. What I had to put up with. He used to knock hell out of me – he put me in hospital once or twice. I had to wait on him hand and foot. When he got back from work, his dinner had to be on the table, or else. But since the strike's been on it's all different. He cleans up now, and washes up. I can go out, and when I come in he'll make a cup of tea for me. I can go and lie down for an hour. I couldn't wish for a better husband, and that's God's truth. And yet before the strike, I sometimes wished him dead, I hated him so much. I shall be sorry when the strike's over, if its only for our own marriage.

Another wrote: 'We actually sit down and talk now. We never used to before.'

And another: 'He said, "I don't know what we'd do without our Rose, because how she's kept us together, God only knows," and that's the first time I've heard him ever compliment me, in 35 years of our marriage.'

One woman, whose husband and son were both miners, had

been agoraphobic, virtually housebound before the strike. Later, she was the hardest worker in the soup kitchen. Another had been an obsessive housewife, always cleaning. But after working for a support group during the strike she had a new system at home: 'Whoever comes in first of an evening does whatever they feel they can do. The house doesn't get cleaned as thoroughly, but we're much happier.' One wife who had been on anti-depressants for 12 years, who was an obsessive weight watcher, a night-time claustrophobic reduced to wandering in the garden in the early hours of the morning 'with nothing logically to be depressed about', was an organiser of fund-raising events during the strike and happy that people had faith in her ability. 'I was asked to do things that a few weeks previously I would not have contemplated.'

About four weeks into the strike it became clear to the North Yorkshire women that it was going to be a long one, and also that something had to be done for the single miners. They were not being given a penny of benefit and would simply have starved if soup kitchens and food parcels had not been started up. There were tales of young men fainting from hunger on the picket lines, and following darts teams from pub to pub so they could get some of the free sandwiches. In fact, most of the first support groups were started up to help the single miners, and only later did they start to feed whole families.

The woman who used to be depressed, finding that she was needed, was suddenly cured.

> I had little confidence but quickly I found that I had some skills that were necessary. I was in at the deep end and this was the antidote. The support group was the best thing that ever happened to me. Consequently I broke the depression and all because of a tragic dispute which gave me reason to stand up and fight.

Another woman wrote:

> I went down for a conference in London, and on the way

back our minibus was full, so I had to hitch a ride with some lasses from Selby. Their spirits were so high, they were singing and shouting all the way. I thought to myself, 'We mustn't ever let these lasses down.' With all the suffering and hardship they've had to live through, their determination was as strong as ever, and it bucked my spirits up no end just to be with them – with people like that on our side I couldn't think of defeat.

Traditionally, working-class women haven't really been allowed to have their own feelings, but a lot of things have changed during the strike . . . I wonder whether Thatcher and MacGregor realise what they've unleashed – they've woken a sleeping bear. I don't think the women will ever go back to the way they were.

The women's opinion of the men was improving – they regarded the strikers with admiration. The North Yorkshire magazine offered this quote: 'One thing this strike's learnt me – it's learnt me he's not too knackered to make love on a night.'

'No, but I am.'

8.
The Miners Come to Town

By the early summer of 1984, signs of real hunger and malnutrition were appearing among children in the pit villages. Only a few pounds a week were coming into most miners' homes, and single miners, mostly young, were getting nothing at all. Schoolteachers and welfare officers were reporting this to no avail. In some areas in Kent, children were even being refused free school meals if their fathers were striking miners. It became clear to people involved with the strike that financial support was urgently needed – and not just support for the pickets which was being organised by the NUM.

Support from London

The collecting boxes were taken into city centres and outside supermarkets. The most generous donations came from London, and to start with it was miners' wives from Kent working with women in London who organised food for the hungry families.

A group working from a tiny portable cabin next to the British Legion in Kennington took over on behalf of the families. Meetings with women from the Kent support groups were organised. Kate Bennett, an organiser for the Southwark trade union support unit, explained how they had asked the miners' wives to prepare a shopping list so the London women knew what to buy with the funds they were raising. The Kent women went back to their villages and asked women what they most needed. The answer was practically everything. 'Don't be too shy or proud,' they were urged. 'Put it all down. Say what you would really like to have.'

Kate Bennett and the other women were shocked when they saw the lists. They had expected requests for small extras and luxuries the women could no longer afford. Instead, the families were asking for bare necessities which showed only too clearly that they were now truly on the breadline. They asked for potatoes and onions and dried milk and razor blades, toilet paper, sanitary towels and tampons. One or two 'extras' were listed for children, who were missing jelly and instant whip. They wanted tea and toothpaste and tinned meat for the pickets' sandwiches. The list for babies was the most shocking: terry towelling nappies, rusks, baby oil, cotton wool and tinned foods, items which, for the past 40 years at least, have been regarded as essentials.

The lists were sent off to all the organisations which had promised help and the first convoy of goods collected and sent to Kent in May 1984 consisted of nine vanloads of food.

A London supporter of the strike told me:

By October 1984 there was a food stand for mining families set up every Saturday about five minutes from where I live in West Hampstead.

At first I bought a lot of fresh food. Greenham women had apparently been suffering from Vitamin C deficiency and there had been cries for oranges and lemons, so I thought I would buy the same for miners and their families. But, as autumn drew into winter, I was horrified to learn they lacked absolute essentials. One week I bought about 20 tins of baby food; another, packets and packets of disposable nappies. Clearly I didn't look like a mother of at least 10 young children for I was asked why I was buying such large quantities. 'For the miners,' I replied. Nobody ever queried why I bought what I bought again.

I aimed to spend £5 per week on food. I was absolutely convinced I had to do this. And this was despite the fact that I was coming across a lot of mindless opposition to the strike from people I was associated with, and would feel very alienated. There was a lot of talk of 'bloody miners', 'holding us up to ransom', 'no understanding of economics', etc.

In Southwark, a borough not noted for its wealth, it was ironically the poorest who demonstrated the greatest generosity. (One in five of Southwark's population was unemployed.) In answer to the women's appeal for food, they brought their weekly shopping straight to the support cabin to be sent to the miners' families.

Much of the support given to the miners' families came from London. Many Londoners remember the miseries and isolation that resulted from the enforced resettlement programme imposed on the East End in the 1950s and 1960s in order to get employment into the regions and to act as a solution to London's postwar housing problems.

Miners' wives took out the collecting boxes and spoke at meetings. It was a cheerfully frenetic time. The organisation was so hurried that sometimes two women would turn up at the same meeting to speak on the same theme. No one minded.

The success achieved by forming the links between Kent and the Southwark groups established a pattern of operating. Collecting points were set up in many other areas and food and money gathered in and then sent to coalfields all over Britain, notably the north-east, Derbyshire and Nottinghamshire.

London money and generosity kept the strike going.

The amount of money and food contributed was so large that the collection was taken over by the Transport and General Workers' Union at Headland House.

Hundreds of thousands of pounds were distributed to miners throughout the country and all the London boroughs which had decided to help them worked from Headland House.

Summer saw the nadir of the strike. The women's march

through London in August 1984 was a lone voice in a capital which had holidays on its mind and was tired of the miners' strike. 'The strike could have quietly died during this time,' Kate Bennett said. 'We knew if we could get through August we might be OK. We kept on collecting in London. We had 500 collectors, so we drew hope from them. Just one pitch could get £1,000 in one day. On average, 20 collectors were getting about £300 each in one day.'

Support from Other Areas

There was scarcely a city or town in Britain which did not contribute in some way to the miners and their families. In Scotland, and in Labour-controlled areas in England and Wales, local authorities gave active support in providing many kinds of assistance. This was often done in the face of angry Tory opposition. In Glasgow, a cabin for food collection was set up in the centre of George Square, opposite the Council Chambers, by members of the district council.

Soon the miners' collection buckets became a familiar feature outside supermarkets everywhere. Sometimes, however, the police would arrest the collectors in the streets – and would also threaten those who gave money to the miners with arrest. Shoppers became frightened of giving money in case they incurred police retribution.

Not Just Tea and Sandwiches

The women found supporters everywhere ready to help them in their new mood of assertiveness and idealism. In Edinburgh, the city's first Labour council mounted an exhibition in October 1984. 'Not just tea and sandwiches' was an exhibition about the work of the women's support groups and the idea had been put forward by the council's newly formed Women's Committee. (The new administration had wanted a socialist exhibition, but the Women's Committee had insisted on an exhibition with a feminist perspective – and the Women's Committee got what they wanted.)

One of the senior museums staff at the City Art Centre said ruefully that in 12 years he had never before had to have meetings with councillors on the staging of an exhibition. The now famous picture of the mounted policeman drawing a baton above Lesley Boulton as she was calling for an ambulance to help an injured miner was put in specifically at the request of a councillor. Some of the staff said the exhibition could raise ethical problems for the staff because it was 'political'. But when it was finally staged it created a major impact. Women from all over Scotland went to see it, and it was taken on tour.

One of the senior staff said women in the strike centres were genuinely surprised that anyone from an art gallery would be interested in what they were doing. 'Once they got over their surprise they were very pleased. I don't think most of them went to museums, and neither did they expect those sort of places to be interested in what they were doing. Instead of dealing with artists or art galleries, as we usually do, we found ourselves dealing with the miners' welfare centres and soup kitchens to get the exhibits and pictures. My great problem was that at the beginning I knew nothing at all about the strike. That soon changed.'

Items exhibited included banners, photographs, and items made by the women to raise funds. Anne Scargill came with Betty Heathfield to the opening, and talked about women's new – or revived – political role.

Public Support

There was a 'reasonable' level of co-operation between the women and the NUM in London, but the women organisers put it no higher than that. It was possible that the NUM felt threatened by the women's sudden and unprecedentedly powerful position.

The NUM could see that the public preferred to give money to the families rather than to the pickets. Though miners were held high in public estimation, people started to get unhappy about pictures now appearing on television of hurled bricks and overturned vehicles, the beating up of a working miner and the attacks on his home. Londoners who were giving donations did not want to get involved in this aspect of the strike and support started to drop away.

However, people did not want to see families starve in what was still supposed to be a welfare state. They did not want to see a drop in living standards to the near starvation level of many people living in the 1930s. So they were still ready to give money, provided they knew it would go direct to the families.

Public support had reacted to the scenes from Yorkshire and Nottinghamshire on television, and the weakening state of the miners, their funds seized by the courts and their food supplies getting scarce. Children were starving. What kind of country was it, people asked, to let children starve? Whatever the reason, there was no doubt that public support was at its highest point just before the miners' leaders themselves brought the strike to an end in March 1985.

Trade Union Support

London's 700,000 trade unionists – the approximate number in 1984 – were all giving to the miners' strike.

But even though the money and food kept on pouring out from London to the coalfields, in the end it was not enough to keep the strike going.

The TUC's promise of support (at the 1984 TUC Congress) was never kept – proving to be only a token gesture – and by the autumn the end of the strike was already in sight. Ironically, it was at that time that the general public began to show more sympathy for the miners and the funds started to flood in, sometimes from very unexpected quarters. But all this was too late.

By Christmas, it was clear that the support in terms of industrial action from the other unions was not going to be forthcoming. There were only generous financial contributions.

The unions were fearful of a repetition of the disaster of the General Strike of 1926 which had failed. The shortage of jobs meant that all trade unionists were now living under the fear of unemployment and a future on the dole. The govenment's new trades union legislation made every union vulnerable to financial ruin if it gave support to the NUM.

The rail unions and the seamen's unions had given support to the strike, refusing to carry imported coal, much of it coming from eastern Europe and South Africa, which kept stocks piled high. In Scotland, for a time there was a rail union ban on the transport of coal from the Scottish pits to the British Steel works at Ravenscraig. Dockers of the Transport and General Workers' Union refused to unload ships at Hunterston bringing imported iron ore for Ravenscraig. However, labour was hired from neighbouring farms and the support collapsed. The steelworkers, fearful about a final closure of Ravenscraig, would not give total support to the miners and, in fact, broke their own production targets during the strike.

There were many instances of supportive industrial action – often individually courageous, particularly among the railwaymen – but they were unco-ordinated and, with the union leaders falling out with each other at national level, were bound to fail.

The Triple Alliance formed for mutual solidarity between the NUM and the rail and steel unions broke down early in the strike.

The bitterness of the breakdown was illustrated by the violent clashes between pickets and police outside Ravenscraig, at the Hunterston iron ore port and at the Orgreave coking plant which supplied the Scunthorpe steel plant, where the picket of 10,000 on 18 June saw the bloodiest day in the strike.

Male trade unionists admitted they had given support to the women's march through London in August 1984 – a watershed in the strike from which the women's groups moved on to greater strength – because of narrow political motives. On the one hand they found the women useful. On the other they were uneasy about their power. The men could no longer do without the women during the strike, but they would have felt happier not to have had to lean on them so heavily. They suspected, with good reason, that it was going to mean trouble for doctrinaire trade unionists after the strike if women continued to insist on their right to a say in the way things were being run.

The Christmas Appeal

The Christmas appeal was a response from some London socialists to the failure of the media to express the undoubted undercurrent of support for the miners nationwide. Why not have a Christmas appeal for the miners' families? The children wouldn't be getting any Christmas unless money were quickly forthcoming.

The appeal was launched through advertisements, initially appearing in the *Guardian* and *Daily Mirror*, and followed up in other newspapers. It was surprisingly successful. The organisers phoned up all the politicians, film stars, academics, writers, rock groups and religious leaders they could think of, and almost all of them said yes to the suggestion they should subscribe and have their names printed on the appeal. Most of the individuals were able to suggest others who could be approached. A pyramid was built up.

The women's support groups were receiving a higher profile in the media, though one of the Chesterfield group said sceptically that this was because everyone knew there was no longer any chance that the strike could be won and so a little sympathy was allowed to sneak in.

One man who signed the appeal said that up until then he had thought of the strike as just another dispute over wages. He happened to have heard a woman from a Durham support group on the radio speaking about the tragedy of the decline of the pit villages. He suddenly saw the situation as the same as the enforced decline and rundown of the docklands communities in

the 1970s, which he himself had experienced. He understood
the point made that a pit village was somewhere you could feel
you belonged, safe in an oasis in the middle of the two-pronged
perils of the recession and a Thatcherite administration. Jobs
down the pits might be hard, but at least they were jobs and not
the dole. It was safer in those pit villages than, for instance,
sleeping over the heating vents in London, which the jobless
from all over the country were now doing every night in the
winter, having 'got on their bikes' to seek work in the capital.
He could see that the women would consider the mines a safer
place for their sons than sleeping rough in the cities.

The Christmas advertisement caught on with the media.
Newspapers other than the *Guardian* and the *Mirror* offered to
carry it at reduced rates. Politics did not seem to enter into it.
There was no obvious common link in the long list of
professors, writers, actors, publishers – some of them normally
numbered among the reactionary. The appeal raised £400,000
in time for Christmas.

Outside the undergrounds, the mainline stations and supermarkets, the notes were still filling collecting buckets. Letters
arrived, too. Even when Christmas had come to an end, Hilary
Wainwright was receiving letters of support for the miners at
the rate of about 50 a day.

Support came from blacks in Toxteth, Brixton and
Chapeltown in Leeds. The print unions – soon to face an
industrial shutdown themselves – went in coachloads to visit the
pit villages and fed whole communities with funds. The
secretary of one such, which took £750 with them to the
north-east, said: 'It was the derelict villages which shook me.
You could see how much they depended on the pit. If the
villages lost the pit they were dead. The new factories which
had been built in the areas around were long since closed.'

The NCB Backlash

Government ministers were put out by the very enthusiastic

response to the Christmas appeal. If this was the way things were going, their case might be lost.

The NCB still had some cards to play, however. The first was a handsome Christmas bonus for any miner who went back to work before Christmas. For some family men the bait was too much. They were sickened by having to accept any more charity, and their families were desperately hard up. In increasing numbers they started to turn up for the early morning shifts. The NCB hardly needed to falsify their return to work figures any longer.

Yet if the miners returning to work had known about the growing support from the general public they might not have felt so defeated.

The February Appeal

The Christmas appeal was followed by a second and similar one. This brought in money just as the strike was being wound up by the NUM leaders.

The second advertisement was a more ambitious affair which described some hitherto unpublished stories from miners' families. 'Every week letters come from miners' families, with newborn babies and sick children who should qualify for special coal allowances. The Coal Board has refused to give these allowances. One NCB area manager summed up the government's attitude when he told a striking miner's wife whose baby was suffering from asthma: "If you want coal, get your husband back to work".'

Whole families have existed on as little as £21 a week for 11 long months. Family savings are spent. Enormous debts have piled up. And children have grown out of worn clothes and battered shoes. 140,000 miners are still on strike. They should not be left alone at this time of greatest need. We are asking you to give every pound you can muster. And we ask you to give right now.

The advertisement added: 'The government has spent £5 billion to drive people to this. £5 billion would cover more than 10 years' subsidy to the NCB.' The point was being made that the suffering had cost as much as retaining the jobs would have done.

The money poured in once more. The appeal to commonsense as well as to humanity was strong. The economic planners of the past, who had created the derelict villages, the disaster of Toxteth, the destruction of the docklands and the transfer of population to the new towns no longer had any credibility, and the monetarists, with their plans to close the pits and instead pay dole money, sounded as though they were soulless elitists. There were many who decided at long last to join the strikers' cause and to opt for the conservation of coal as a fuel power. It was too late. The advertisement went out on February 27 1985. The end of the strike was only seven days away.

One miner's wife in Lothian, Scotland, put the position very succinctly: 'A lot of people have been saying against us that we think we've a God-given right to jobs, while other people are losing theirs. It's not that. We don't want something for nothing, we really don't. We want a chance for our children and other people's children. Just a chance.'

'Everybody deserves a chance,' said her friend. 'Not to be thrown on the scrap heap before you've started.'

9.
Winter

There is a steep bank above the Barony pit in Ayrshire where, if you scrabble with your hands, you can find coal. During the strike there were always people there, searching for some fuel – it is known as 'scratting' – to make a fire and relieve the cold that was starting to make them feel ill. The cold of a Scottish winter is always harsh and can make people feel sick as well as bring about lack of energy and will. Many thousands of people in Scotland in all-electric council flats in the towns are without heating in winter as a matter of course – because they cannot afford it. Now the miners had joined that group.

One man had been killed in a fall down the Ayrshire bank a month before Christmas 1984. Even so, people were back again a few days later still looking for coal. As darkness fell (about 4 pm at that time of the year) one man came down from the bank. 'Look,' he said. 'Three bags, that's all, and I've been here all day.' His wife had a job, he said, so they were not so badly off as some. His boy was doing well at the local academy and taking his O levels. He hoped the son would be able to get out of all this misery if he did well enough at school. In the meantime he was coming out every day, trying to pick up enough coal to make a fire for when his family got home at night. He was sure about the rightness of the strike. He would not picket, but he was not going back.

The Cold

A number were killed during the strike, trying to get coal for their fires. Electricity and gas were cut off because they could not pay the bills. Outsiders tended to believe press stories that they were doing it for the money. 'They're stealing coal and then selling it.'

They did not seem to understand that miners' families were desperate with the cold. If the police saw them taking coal they would simply grab the sack they carried it in and arrest them. After a court appearance the NCB would probably sack them. The old, the sick and the very young were supposed to get 'concessionary' coal from the NCB, but some doctors refused to supply the certificates they needed to get it.

One woman in Barnsley was nursing a rich little seam she had found beneath a patch of ground where they were starting to build houses. Miners' families have a feel for coal and where it is – like water diviners for water. It is often lying near the surface in mining areas but is hidden for ever once building on the land starts. The woman was determined to get this coal for her stove, for she had been without fuel for days. The seam was six feet deep, and it would make all the difference to Christmas. She took her teenage son with her. He was planning to go into the navy and was taking exams and did not want to get into any trouble with the police. But he was not going to let his mother go by herself. So, after dark, they set off together, armed with a shovel.

She dug hard and soon had a sack filled. Scaffolding had been put up where they were building the new houses and she told her son to climb up and sit on it and keep a lookout for the police. If he gave a warning she could get away quickly before she was caught. Nobody wanted the coal and it would soon be covered up by the builders, but she was scared.

She was so absorbed in her work and so pleased with her seam, that she did not notice in the darkness that her son had got down from the scaffolding. He had seen a policeman coming. He knew that his mother might get off, but he also knew that if he were caught he would get worse treatment. He scarpered, calling to his mother as he went. She understood. She wasn't angry with him, but she was scared out of her wits when the policeman appeared in front of her. He stood and looked at her for a long time and at the coal, and he was shaken. All he said was: 'I'm sorry to see someone like you having to do this.' Then he took the coal from her and they went back together. There was no talk of her having to go to the police station. All she said to me about that was: 'It was a pity, it was such a lovely seam.'

The hardness of the winter, the cold at home and the lack of food or any comforts were beginning to take their toll on people's health. Some miners went back, but most of the families were still determined to stay out as Christmas approached. They saw it as a war which was intended to break them, and they could not give in. They thought that if they went under, there would be nothing but the dole ahead. Robert Gillespie, the secretary of the West of Scotland branch of SOGAT, one of the print unions, which did more than other unions to keep families fed, said to me about this time: 'They're just living on beans and toast. The parents are run down, the children are starting to have boils and showing all the signs of malnutrition.'

Usually the families were too proud to tell any outsider what their way of living was like. They would not even tell each other. One miner would notice telltale signs that a young neighbour was desperate for food for his children and he would slip him a loaf without saying anything at all. Robert Gillespie said he had heard about the hardship in the summer, when they had taken the wives and children away to their convalescent home for a holiday. Once the children were in bed, they would open the bar and give the wives a drink. 'That was when the tears started to flow and they told us what it was really like.' Since then, of course, winter had arrived and things had become much worse.

One Durham wife described what the cold was like.

Around Christmas time the cold nearly defeated us. I remember New Year's Eve. I had bronchitis, and it was freezing. We had bits of plastic covering the walls to keep the cold out. I was lying in bed to get warm and my husband came through with a free bottle of sherry that he'd won in a raffle. He says, 'Look, do you want a drink?' But I says 'No, I want to die.' The cold, the cold. My bones were sore. I think people couldn't stand the cold. We had no coal, nobody had any coal.

We all thought if we got over Christmas – that's the worst time, the testing time – we'd be all right. Before Christmas there was just a handful of men going in. Then after Christmas they just fled in; they ran in.

They wanted to get warm again.

The Lack of Food

At the strike centre in Chesterfield in Derbyshire a long queue of striking miners waited for their food parcels. They found it demeaning, but at least it was something they could do for their wives, who often lived miles away from the centre and were burdened with young children. The bare strike centre just before Christmas was a shock. Until then, I had still assumed that there was a welfare state in Britain for those in need. That belief disappeared for me when I saw miners at the back of the hall packing tins of baby food into the food parcels. There were only three or four baby food tins in each parcel for a whole week. What did babies eat the rest of the time? Cornflakes?

In some cases miners were having to look after the babies themselves. One woman had been forced to stop breastfeeding her baby because she was so hungry and short of food that she had no more milk. Another had been sent to stay in hospital by her doctor, even though she had children to care for. If she did not go to hospital, he had said he would not answer for the consequences. She was suffering from malnutrition, and she was also being physically damaged by the constant cold. It was not just old people who were suffering and dying from hypothermia in the winter of 1984; miners' families were as well.

The queue would move slowly towards the desk in the centre of the hall of the Chesterfield strike centre. Occasionally a man would break away and go round the back to where the miners were packing the parcels. 'They come around and whisper to us that they need extra because they've got a big family,' said one of the parcel-packers. 'They're too embarrassed to ask in front of the others, too proud. We always try to give them a bit extra. Some of them have four or five children.'

All the parcels were the same, and although they were intended for a whole week, one person with a healthy appetite could have demolished the lot in a day. The men waiting for the parcels looked drawn, depressed and hungry.

It seemed unbelievable that in London – and, in fact, only a few miles away in Chesterfield – one individual would be paying out the money which an entire miner's family had to live on for a whole month on just one meal in a restaurant.

The weekly food parcel list consisted of: One packet of cereal, one small tin of soup, one small tin of corned beef or other meat, one small tin of peas, one of baked beans, two pounds of sugar and two lots of fresh vegetables, a few tins of baby food, some sanitary towels, shampoo and nappies. In many of the surrounding areas in Derbyshire there were no soup kitchens. In any case, people had no means of reaching them. Where there were soup kitchens, meals were being provided two or three times a week only, not every day as in other mining areas.

The Derbyshire Women's Action Group

Just before Christmas 1984, the Derbyshire Women's Action Group put out a statement headed: 'Guts and Principles'. It read:

We have nothing but admiration for the courage of these men and their families who remain solidly behind their principles in fighting for their jobs and their communities. We feel our men have more guts than those who are bribed by their own money to become scabs, and have to hide behind wire mesh and crawl back on their knees.

They will never know what it will be like to walk into work with dignity as we shall when our fight is won.

We shall make every effort to ensure your children have presents and food for Christmas. YOUR WOMEN SUPPORT YOU AND THANK YOU FOR OUR CHILDREN'S FUTURE.

There was no doubt the men were touched.

Betty Heathfield, who had been much involved in the Derbyshire Women's Action Group, was particularly respected. She seemed tireless. She knew everybody, every problem, every detail of the food supplies.

At the same time she was working hard as a national speaker, fund raising for the striking miners. She did not often get the chance to see her husband, Peter Heathfield, the general secretary of the NUM. She also led the women's action group constantly on the picket lines.

The Barnsley Women Against Pit Closures

According to 'Women against pit closures', one of a series of booklets published during and after the strike by the Barnsley women, an important element that led to the formation of the Barnsley Women Against Pit Closures was the anger at the way in which the newspapers had initially depicted women as being against the strike. They wrote in this first issue:

A spate of reports had sought to portray women, and miners' wives in particular, as victims of the irresponsible action taken by the NUM.

Women have always been presented as being passive and quiet, unable to organise anything other than housework. The early months of the miners' strike have smashed that myth; women have demonstrated their ability to organise to an extent that the press could no longer ignore.

Some women in the Barnsley Women Against Pit Closures support group felt that unless concessions to the women were gained during the strike, they would have no chance of winning them once the strike was over.

The Barnsley Panel was a powerful discussion forum for miners and their leaders, formed in the 1960s by Arthur Scargill, which had widespread influence in the NUM. Politically active women in BWAPC wanted to join the Barnsley Panel and take part in the discussions. They were, after all, a vital part of the strike machinery. It turned out, however, that the Barnsley Panel – with some exceptions, including Arthur Scargill – were willing to give very little space to these women, even though they recognised the vital role they were playing.

Women's group members taking part in strike meetings, according to the miners, talked trivialities too much and looked bored when they were discussing technical mining and union matters. It was to remedy this that the women started on their political education. They started to educate themselves in the shorthand of the political and industrial world, so that they could take an equal part in meetings.

They had some success.

It was the desire of one section of the BWAPC to play a more responsible political role that partly led to a split within the organisation in December 1984. Anne Scargill, the wife of the NUM President, helped to form a separate women's group, a breakaway from the original BWAPC, to maintain a more traditional women's place. The split caused the women's support system to wobble around the critical weeks before Christmas, at a time when the demands on the women were heaviest and when the NUM leadership were already aware of the date the strike might end. However, the break was patched up and the organisations carried on together throughout the Christmas period and are now united under the Women Against Pit Closures banner.

Christmas 1984

Christmas was the sternest trial of all for the miners' wives. They could have coped with the lack of Christmas celebrations and the children's expectations of presents being unsatisfied. Children's attitudes are endlessly flexible, and can accommodate those they love: their parents. No one had to explain the difficulties to the children. They had the largest collections of miners' strike badges, played 'scabs and pickets' in the playground and demanded to be taken on demonstrations and marches wearing miners' helmets. From a child's point of view, Christmas 1984 was not a bad substitute for a normal Christmas. Father Christmas was a scab, they said. If he brought you a present, it meant you were a scab, too. In that way, they adapted to the deprivations they suffered.

It was the sheer organisational demands of a massive communal miners' Christmas, with a bankrupt union and rapidly dwindling funds, which caused the women the greatest stress.

At the best of times Christmas is a hard time for women. Most resent its materialism, its commercialism, and its almost total departure from any link with the Christianity which gave its name to the festival. They resent the hard work, the lack of leisure, the constant feeling of money being tight, the waste and the ridiculous over-abundance of food in a starving world. Women only talk about these things privately to each other. It is a man's festival, fostered by men, who organise the big works get togethers and office parties, and pretend they are doing this for the women.

Women enjoy giving presents to their children, but the best present anyone could give them would be some time to themselves, the one gift they never get. It is, no doubt, their frustration at Christmas that results in the rise in divorce rates afterwards!

Multiply the stress by a thousand times or so, and you are near to understanding what the organisers of the women's support groups were going through before Christmas 1984. The non-organisers, with their meagre food parcels and cold houses and scarcely a drink to cheer them up, had a hard time, but many had families in work in jobs other than mining, who invited them round for Christmas Day.

Charitable people, who had been preoccupied with starvation in Ethiopia during the previous two months, woke up to the fact that the striking miners and their families were also not going to have any Christmas dinner and toys. The plan was to get every miner's family a Christmas dinner. In Scotland, a food convoy of 10,000 chickens was delivered to the mining areas by SOGAT. In Chesterfield, Kate Whitehead snapped up an offer of hundreds of frozen chickens. Offers to provide food and toys started to flood in.

Jean McCrindle, handling cheques for the miners' families Christmas appeal, said that the main problem had been getting the cheques with which she and her helpers were engulfed cleared through the banks in time for the money to be translated into food and toys. Her team worked hard to get the money through, but a week before Christmas at least £150,000 had still not been cleared, though the banks, Jean said, were as helpful as they could be.

For the organisers, their own family demands and particular problems related to Christmas Day had to be put to one side as they had to cope with the vast food and clothing distribution in the strike centres.

In the pit villages, food, money and toys arrived only a few days before Christmas Eve.

The logistics of the organisation were impossible.

'The trouble is,' confided one delegate at Bilston Glen colliery, 'we've got these 100,000 toys coming from France. But we don't know exactly when they are coming or how we are going to distribute them when they do.'

At the miner's welfare at Fallin, the tiny Stirlingshire village opposite Polmaise colliery, the toys were brought in by miners in an unwieldy convoy.

The French trade unionists had done a marvellous job in buying the toys. They were all good quality and they had been chosen with Gallic imagination. The trouble was that they ranged from toy railways to rattles, from bicycles to balloons. In a small village how could you possibly share out fairly and not cause jealousy? The women had been hoping that the toys would arrive in time for them to think about them all carefully, and to allocate a toy to each child in a way that would not leave others feeling deprived. And they all had to be wrapped. Sleepless, the already worn out women of Fallin stayed up all night during the weekend to sort out the toys which had been dumped hurriedly in a room in the miners' welfare. Finally they realised that they were going to be able to achieve nothing more ambitious than a high-class bran tub for the children. Even so, somehow they managed to distribute all the presents.

The Beginning of the End

The strain was starting to show. All the striking miners' centres had Christmas parties. But it was a time when exhaustion caused disagreements among people who previously had been getting along with each other like soldiers together in a trench or patients in a hospital ward. What was now being asked of the women was just too much. And it did not help that they were aware all the time that for other families in other places, Christmas was not like this. Even the ones who were being entertained by their families who were outside the mining industry could not help contrasting their own state with the comparative wealth of grandparents, aunts and uncles and even sometimes sons and daughters – who had money to spend and plenty of food and drink in the house. It is no fun suddenly finding out you are deprived.

It gave the miners' families a better understanding of what it was like to be unemployed, and it was the unemployed who were now among their strongest allies and most regular supporters on the picket lines.

'We had the feeling that if we could just get over Christmas, we could carry on the strike indefinitely,' said a miner's wife at Easington colliery in Durham. 'Once it was over, we heaved a sigh of relief. We thought, "Well, we've survived that, so we can survive anything." That was one reason we were so broken up when the strike ended suddenly in March.'

It was no accident that more men were going back to work after Christmas, and in steadily increasing numbers, than they had done before when the NCB was holding out the allure of a handsome Christmas bonus. Miners were able to stand the hardship but not the kindness and charity. They themselves had always looked after the weak through the miners' lodges. They weren't used to being categorised as weak themselves. And now that the NUM had cut down on the picketing, they were beginning to feel outcasts. Christmas and charity were the last straw. Bitterly, they went back to work, often in the face of pleading on the part of their wives not to do so.

A wife on the Monktonhall Women's Support Committee in Scotland said she could not stomach the fact that a young neighbour who was a miner, to whom she had given Christmas food and brand new clothes for his baby, had accepted them all gratefully, and then, a few weeks later, had gone back to work – whereas he had always up until then been solidly behind her husband, a member of the strike committee.

For a short time after Christmas, there was a final burst of picketing. Miners and their wives, together with the unemployed and peace and pressure groups, turned up throughout the coalfields. There was not much publicity and no violence. The media were not told about the mass pickets in advance, and they did not seem to want to know. The media generally were now simply waiting for the strike to end.

The signs were all there. Early in the year, the secret talks with management started in Wales to see what deals could be made when a return to work was started. During a mass rally in

George Square in Glasgow on a freezing day in February, George Bolton, the Deputy President of the Scottish NUM, reported that he had just had a successful meeting with the Secretary of State for Scotland, George Younger, a senior member of Mrs Thatcher's Cabinet. Mr Younger had been quite sympathetic, he said. He had promised to pass on the miners' views on pit closures to the Cabinet. The Church of Scotland, and other churches which had organised dawn visits to the picket lines, were on the miners' side about the economic arguments against pit closures. Someone like George Younger would have to take notice of the Church of Scotland, he said. Nothing could have spelt out so clearly the miners' defeat as Bolton's eager grasping of these straws.

Later, Mick McGahey made a speech to the assembled miners. He adjured them, in fine nineteenth-century rhetoric, to stand 'shoulder to shoulder, heads high'. But the rally was more like a wake.

McGahey seemed to be thanking them all for their fortitude during the strike, telling them they had written an unforgettable chapter in industrial history. Coupled with George Bolton's unexpected empathy with George Younger and the Scottish churches, it seemed, in spite of the cheers in George Square, to mark the end.

One month later, the strike was officially over.

10.
The End of the Strike

The death pangs were terrible. The sacked miners and the women, for the most part, could not believe the NUM intended to give in. South Wales had decided to vote with those coalfields deciding to go back, at the vital meeting at Congress House on 3 March 1985. That settled it. The vote of the delegates was narrow – 98–91 in favour of going back – and the South Wales motion only just defeated Yorkshire, after hours of angry debate.

Some Welsh miners blamed the communists among the leadership for ending the strike, because they feared they would be discredited and torn apart if they went on further to certain defeat. 'The Communists led the way back because they were scared of losing their leadership,' said one Welsh delegate, a comment which was repeated among Scottish miners.

Yorkshire and Scotland wanted to carry on the strike until the pits which the NCB had threatened to close – Bullcliffe Wood (Yorkshire), Polmaise (Scotland), Snowdown (Kent), Herrington (North East) and Cortonwood (Yorkshire) – were promised a future, and until the sacked miners had been given an amnesty. Given that the rebellion of the miners against the government's policies had started at those pits, and had sparked off the strike, and that some of the sacked miners had committed extremely minor offences, it seemed a minimum demand. But it was not to be met.

Patrick Wintour of the *Guardian* reported the scenes outside Congress House when the news of the vote was given and he described a scene of sheer disbelief and grief. The Scots from Polmaise and Monktonhall had sent down coachloads of sacked miners for the occasion – 'We're not going to let them forget we are here,' the Scots delegates had said.

Wintour's report said that as Arthur Scargill came out to confirm the news that the strike had ended: 'Voices from Wales, Scotland and Yorkshire screamed at their leader, "Arthur, you've been betrayed", "Give us leadership", "We cannae go back".'

The Scottish miners were the most emotional. Apart from everything else, they had the additional anger of feeling yet another English betrayal. One of the Scottish miners screamed out at the walls of the Congress House:

We've given you our hearts, we've given you blood, we've given you everything and then you sell us out. Davie Jones and Joe Green died on the picket line for this and you turn round and slap us in the face with a great big fish. We'll never go back to work. You're tarred and feathered with the rest of the scabby bastards.

Then he collapsed in tears.

John Swain, a Polmaise miner, was stunned: 'I've been sacked for rushing a police officer . . . The judge has just given me a reprimand but I'm still sacked. And what have I done? I fought for my job. Why should we go back? We've been out for 12 months and we've got nothing. What sort of a decision is this?'

In the pit villages, the scenes had been even more traumatic than outside Congress House. The women were continuing with the support groups. There were plans for a big women's rally the following week. So far as the women were concerned, though they knew a vote was to be taken, it was inconceivable the strike could end now, before the future of the threatened pits had been secured, without at least some consultation with them, the women who had kept the strike going.

It was a day of weeping, for men as well as women. In Nottinghamshire, where a minority had faced violent opposition from working miners, the feelings were bitter. Elsie Lowe at Clipstone said: 'We just saw the end of the strike as a sell out. Nottinghamshire had been left out on a limb.'

Almost universally the women were against the miners going back to work. They had not suffered a whole year's privations and hardship to give in then. They begged the miners not to return, saying they could hang on longer to support them. But, in the final analysis, they had no vote and no real voice. They came face to face with reality. They were not part of the economic unit of the pits, and had no influence on the decision about when the strike should end. They were not miners.

The Return to Work

Once down the mines again, faced with the pit managers' deliberately humiliating behaviour, with threats of being sacked and with more pit closures, men went home at the end of a shift in no mood to discuss sharing nights out with their wives. In any case, most of them did not relish going back down underground. In a job almost intolerable at the best of times, miners keep going by maintaining the unbroken routine of going down for the shift, and keeping up the teamwork spirit with their mates. Going back down out of the daylight meant money, food and beer again, but the return was as painful for them as it was for their wives.

'We're not going back,' one supporter shouted at Phil Bowen, delegate from Blaenant colliery in south Wales, as he left a meeting in Cardiff. 'It's all right for you, love, you don't have to,' he shouted back.

Many of the women in the support groups could not believe that the strike was actually over. After all they had been through they regarded it as treachery on the part of the NUM as, in fact, did the sacked miners who were now left stranded.

(In Edinburgh, Mick McGahey was physically assaulted by miners as he came out of the final executive meeting to announce that they were going back to work.)

It was this conviction which made the women beg the men not to return to work, even after the final executive meeting in London had decided to call an end to the strike. They wept. They could not believe that their sacrifices might have been all for nothing.

In the end, the women led the marches back to work all over Britain, with bands and banners. They were not, they said, going to have the men crawling back on hands and knees to the government.

There were to be kilts and pipers in Scotland and bands in Wales, flags and cheering to mask the rockbottom spirits. It certainly had more to do with strategy than outright defeat. But at least the strikers still had enough heart in them to march with the women back to the pits with music playing.

The women did not think they had been defeated and, once they had accepted the strike was over, they put a brave face on it. There would be no safety for the family in defeat, it was true. Everyone was now fair game for persecution. But a bold front might help.

Mary Parry, Murton Wives Support Group in County Durham, said: 'It sounds silly, but on the day it was the women who carried the banner back. We led the men. It was something that had never ever been done. We never had anything to do with that banner before. Even some of the women thought that we shouldn't have been carrying it because that was miners' history.'

Her husband, Johnnie, had been at the final meeting at Congress House: 'I could say many things about it, but I'm not going to,' he said.

Mary was left at home while he went to the meeting. One of the strike committee phoned her to tell her the news. The man couldn't speak properly because he started weeping and could not get the words out. That made Mary cry. 'We were both just standing there, crying on the phone, not able to say anything.

All the lads in the village were crying. It was a terrible day.'

Not all the pits were willing to go back as the NUM had directed. They drifted back over a period of a week, pit by pit. For instance, it was a full week after the directive before Bilston Glen in Scotland went back, after having had the nod from David Hamilton, the pit delegate who had been imprisoned and sacked. They went back with pipes playing Scotland the Brave, with the women in the forefront of the march.

The End of the Strike

Before the strike, miners at Maerdy colliery in Wales were already very short of money. The pit had been 19 weeks without overtime pay because of the NUM ban on overtime. The determination to fight to keep the pit open, however, was rock solid. 'There's been no new machinery in Maerdy in ten years,' said Babs Williams. 'There's no investment; the pit has been starved. Put back the 1,470 men they've taken away, and the machinery and they would soon get their economic coal.'

Not a single miner returned to work during the strike. But, as the strike dragged on, two men were known to be thinking about it, and this was thought to be so extraordinary that Maerdy decided the time must be right to go back. Once Maerdy decided to return, that was it. The rest of the South Wales coalfield knew that if Maerdy was showing even the slightest sign of giving in, that had to mark the end.

'Once you start thinking about going back, you are almost back and in the end you go back,' said one of the Maerdy miners. 'It's the thought that counts.'

So the South Wales leaders started to do quiet deals with the NCB bosses in Wales. By the time they got to Congress House for the last meeting on the Sunday before the end of the strike, the decision had been taken and the conditions for going back to work had been made individually with pit managers. It was the South Wales vote which swung other militant coalfields in favour of the final decision to end the strike, amidst heartbroken cries of 'sell out' from the sacked miners and tears from men and women who had not expected the end to be so abrupt, and with so little consultation at grassroots level.

One of the reasons the women felt the miners should not be going back was because 20 Maerdy men were still on court charges and were almost certain to be found guilty of minor offences on the picket line, such as breach of the peace. Serious offences, which had gained publicity in the strike, had been rare. And the Rhondda people knew that these men on minor offences were likely to be sacked – though in the end none of them was. There was now no chance of striking in support of their reinstatement. They reckoned they had let their fellow miners down, but there was nothing they could do, now. They felt like traitors – and a bit like scabs, too. It was no wonder they could not bear to talk to reporters.

So far as Maerdy miners were concerned, when the end of the strike came, their minds were made up, and they went back to the colliery with the maximum amount of pride and the minimum of fuss.

The men marched back to work singing, with the women at the head with their banners. The women had been asked to lead the march back in tribute to the support they had given. Nobody at Maerdy colliery wanted to end the strike, but, equally, nobody could see any other option. People were crying in the streets as the men returned. The miners applauded the women as they marched. But it was against their will that the men were going back.

What angered the marchers was the behaviour of the television crews and the reporters who gathered round the Maerdy procession which went through the streets with banners and children in pushchairs. They seemed like vultures in at the death.

Reporters pushed round them asking questions. Journalists were making their first appearance in the Rhondda for many months, and this infuriated the women. They did not realise it was not the reporters' fault, nor that of the television crews. Few editors had been interested in discovering what was going on in the pit villages, particularly one as remote as Maerdy. 'The TV reporters didn't know how near they came to being hit,' said one wife. 'They kept jostling us, saying "How does it feel to be going back?" How did they think it felt? People were crying; it was taking all our strength to do it. And none of them had been around during the strike asking how it felt to be on strike, how it felt not to have any food in the house or any fires, or never to go out for a drink. We would have welcomed them then.'

The attitude of the press made them furious. 'They showed a complete turnaround, once we went back. Six months ago we were thugs. No one had a good word to say for us. Then, suddenly, there we were on the television screens being shown as heroes. It made us angry.'

Maerdy is finally closed. But the new spirit born in the women during the strike will not die, and this spirit has been passed on to their children.

Their Heads Held High

The Kent miners went up to picket in Yorkshire – at the request of some Yorkshire miners who did not want to go back. But at the prospect of continuing chaos, the Yorkshiremen asked the Kent miners to stop picketing. Then the Kent miners themselves returned, the last to do so.

For the women at least it was a victory, not a defeat. They had found their political voice and from that time onwards they intended to use it. The women's place in the history of the mining industry was secure. Apart from the suffragettes' struggle for votes for women and the long vigil of endurance by women outside the Greenham Common cruise missile base, this had probably been the most united and sustained women's struggle ever known in Britain.

11.
Never the Same Again

It was not too long before the worst fears of mining communities were being proved right. The miners had, in fact, got nothing – and less than nothing. Within weeks of the end of the strike, the roll call of closures started – in Yorkshire, Wales, Durham and Scotland.

The NCB treated the women's support groups' pleas for the miners sacked during the strike for picketing with an extraordinary lack of compassion. Did newspaper leader writers, who had believed in the NCB statements during the strike, remember how their spokesmen had said there would be no compulsory redundancies? As the announcement came of new closures over and above those expected during the strike – at Emley Moor in Yorkshire and at Frances colliery in Fife – the overseers' union, NACODS, was outraged. NUM members were faced with provocation and discrimination by managers, once they were down the pits again. They were not, however, surprised. They had known that things would be rough – and they expected them to get rougher.

'Men are being penalised because they were on strike and now they are down the pits again,' said John Lowe, picket manager at Clipstone colliery the week after the strike ended.

Down the pits men have work problems they need to discuss with union officials. The work they are being asked to do may be too hazardous or they may have back trouble and not be able to do a particular job. This is where the pit union men are useful. Now, however, said John Lowe, pit managers were starting their own 'work committees' and telling men they should consult these rather than their own union officials. The miners were scared of losing their jobs if they objected to this arrangement. Much of the solidarity had gone and the miners were having a miserable time. 'There are fights and disagreements and the NCB men pick on the ones they know had been striking for the smallest thing. It will never be the same again,' said one Monktonhall wife to me.

Thousands of jobs went in the first few months after the strike, with thousands more to come until the number of closures achieved was beyond even Ian MacGregor's dreams. By June 1985, the NCB (by then renamed British Coal) had plans to lose 25,000 jobs, as the first step in the closure of 70 pits.

In spite of miners' delegates' brave talk that they would fight for the sacked miners once they were back down the pits, the sacked men were not all reinstated. Those back at work had too many problems of their own to be able to fight effectively for others. One wife of the Eppleton Support Group in Hetton described it:

The men look at the conditions they're working in at the pit now, and then they look at the redundancy money. They're working under the whip. My husband used to really love his job, but now he gets his orders changed every two hours. There's no dignity any more and I think the weaker ones are thinking, 'Give me the money and let's get out'. And some of them even say 'Give us me cards and I'll get out', even without the money. They even get sacked for saying 'scab'. The scabs are protected and the strikers are not. My husband loved his job. It sounds soppy but he really loved it. I remember, at 15 years old, he said he wanted to be a shaft man and he eventually became one. Now he goes up there to get the pittance he's earning, £79 a week from five shifts. It would be more, except the NCB are now taking double loan money off us for heating during the strike. I've got a friend with two kids whose husband brings home only £65 now. We've always lived on overtime but there's none now. We had about £130 to £140 a week before the strike. But on the other hand, my husband's a lot healthier now because he gets Saturday and Sunday off.

Throughout the British coalfields the returning miners were telling the same story. In the shadows were the sacked and imprisoned miners, who no longer even had the option of taking redundancy. Many of them had been high-earning face-workers, pit delegates, the leaders. Now they realised they were nothing. They were not even heroes any more.

There were a great many families left with permanent scars. Seven miners had been killed, four of them on picket lines, and 7,000 had been injured, many seriously. Some had been in intensive care and would be damaged for life. At one point nearly 200 were in prison, and 11,000 miners and their wives and supporters had been arrested and detained, many for minor offences.

Quite a number of the imprisoned were miners' leaders. Peter Hogg, of the Scottish NUM executive, had five sons arrested and taken to court, two of whom were sacked. David Hamilton, the chairman of the strike committee at Bilston Glen, went to prison on remand, after a fight in the miners' welfare though he was found not guilty of any offence in court later on. He lost his job.

A year after the strike had ended, in March 1986, nearly 500 miners, sacked from their jobs because they had been arrested on picket lines, were still out of work. (Scotland had only half as many miners as the rest of Britain, but had four times as many strike-related Coal Board dismissals.)

Many of the militant pits had been closed. Even so, in late 1986, nearly two years after the end of the strike, women in the support groups were still raising funds for the sacked miners and their families. The women had decided to fight to re-open the pits that had been closed. The miners found them as solidly organised and as effective in pressing the case for miners' rights and for keeping pits open as they had been during the strike. 'We'll never stop campaigning for justice for miners and their families,' said Ann Lilburn, a miner's daughter, a miner's wife and the mother of two young miners from Northumberland, and the new leader of the Women Against Pit Closures after the strike. She was burning with indignation as she talked about the way the miners' traditional teamwork underground, which involved looking after each other and relying on each other's skills, was being deliberately shattered. In 1986 the miners were still being sacked for trivialities – for being late, for asking for their shifts to be changed – and were being downgraded to jobs paying just over the dole rate.

Many of the miners had been dismissed for alleged offences to which they pleaded not guilty, before their cases had been considered in the courts, when they were still technically innocent. Some were dismissed for alleged offences deemed by the NCB to be 'serious offences' and grounds for dismissal, even though the courts had refused to prosecute on the grounds that there was no case to answer.

Many were dismissed for 'breach of the peace' and 'obstruction' which drew minimum fines and where men had done nothing more than shout or stand on the 'wrong' side of the road.

They are treading on eggshells. We'll go on working for the sacked miners and their families – some of them lost their jobs because a policeman didn't like their faces or they were standing on the wrong side of a white line when they were pickets.

There was the famous case at Bilston Glen in Scotland where a miner – a union official – had stepped over the white line which separated NCB property from municipal property. It was claimed the white line had been newly painted and his defence in court claimed that he was on public property. The man was sacked.

Many of the cases went to Industrial Tribunals under the heading of wrongful dismissal. But even when the tribunals found in favour of the miners, as they often did, the men were still not taken back to their jobs.

It meant they lost any pension rights and, even more important, not only the weekly wage and probably an NCB house, but the right to opt for high redundancy payments being offered by the NCB.

The sacked miners, losing the dole after a year, were living with their families at subsistence level. The miners' wives and their supporters would never forget them. Ann Lilburn and her family had had £6.45 to live on each week during the strike, like many other families; she knew all about malnutrition.

Women Against Pit Closures now plunged themselves into fund-raiding efforts for these miners and their families. Some of the miners were in prison serving comparatively long sentences for lesser crimes, and they became the heroes of the women's movement.

Funds have had to be found, families supported and encouraged, and an immense amount of paper work coped with to secure benefits, representation and the men's rights.

There were also the crippling debts all striking miners had to face after the strike. The funds coming in from the public were very quickly slowed down and stopped, but the financial problems the communities faced were just as bad as they had been during the strike. Frozen fuel bills, rents and hire purchase agreements, or frozen mortgages, now had to be paid. Household maintenance, such as painting and decorating, was now badly in arrears and for a time these had to take priority. Children were developing problems at school – they had been put on the back burner for too long.

Despite all the troubles, I never heard a woman say she regretted having supported the long strike. On the contrary, the miners' wives seemed desperate to keep the spirit that had seen them through the long months, the solidarity and friendship and, above all, the feeling that together they could do something to change the world and make it a better place, not only for themselves, but for all those suffering injustice.

Women Against Pit Closures started to collect ideas from the women's groups about future policy. There was a determination to develop a good working relationship with the NUM at every level and the aim has become not just to maintain links with supporters which were made during the strike, but to extend these links to many other potential supporters, both in Britain and internationally.

The women were to establish the link between the closing of the pits – which were safe and provided jobs – with the desperate Tory rush to open nuclear power stations. The organisation called Links was set up in the New Year of 1986 by a group of miners' wives. Some of these women became extremely well travelled and had world-wide contacts.

Anne Suddick, from Northumberland and one of the founders of Links, organised demonstrations against nuclear power with women from the Greenham Common cruise missile base in Berkshire. They also made connections with Friends of the Earth, Greenpeace and other environmental groups and sympathetic politicians in a vast anti-nuclear power movement. Their first petition collected 50,000 signatures within a few weeks. 'Our message is that there is no hiding place from nuclear power, no escape from a disaster like Chernobyl, for anyone,' said Anne Suddick. 'We want a sane and safe energy policy, not one that costs human lives, deforms babies and causes leukaemia in children.'

Once the men were back, the women quite suddenly found they had no time for committees and for travelling. At the meetings a week or two after the strike ended, invitations from Europe, from Iceland, the Scandinavian countries, almost any part of the globe, were still coming in, asking for miners' wives to go to speak about the miners' strike, with expenses paid. There were offers of holidays for the children abroad. No one seemed able to take these up. 'Everyone is even busier now the strike is over,' said Babs Williams at Maerdy Colliery. 'Now the men are back on the shifts, we have to be at home to get their meals for them. What with that and trying to carry on the committees, we are more tied than ever.'

The problem when the strike ended was that once the men were back down the pits the old patterns were reasserted by force of circumstance. The women's lives once more revolved around shift times and the provision of meals, with the shifts varying from day to day. This left the women little time to do anything else than cope with their lives at home. The support of other women in the soup kitchens had gone and they were left tied to their individual homes. The children were coming home rather than going to the kitchens, and had to be met and given meals.

The women realised it was going to be impossible to achieve their aims, isolated as they were in the small pit villages, unless they could retain not only their own solidarity but also the practical support of the men. The men were once more down the pits, and having to face their own struggles against victimisation. The women had to face the eternal dilemma of the conflict between the existing day-to-day responsibilities of their home lives and the urge to use their brains to cope with the wider issues of the world. And once the adrenalin engendered by the struggle to keep the pits open was not needed any longer after the strike had ended, the women had a deep longing to have a rest, to relax and to recover from their exhaustion. 'I just can't keep going any longer,' was typical of how women felt. But some of the support groups did keep going and it was the meeting of the continuing support groups which brought the women through into the new campaigns.

'We've met people we would never have met if it had not been for the strike,' said Lynn Clegg. 'We get letters now from people all over the world. If we can keep those people interested we can keep the support groups going. We don't want to pack it in.'

Phil Bowen, delegate from Blaenant colliery in South Wales, was sympathetic to the idea of men taking more share in the responsibility of the home, so that women could develop the skills they had learnt during the strike as well as educate themselves. There was now no gainsaying their talent for communication and the ease with which they mixed with other people and achieved results in half the time it took most men to gather support or raise funds. But Phil Bowen was typical of many in the NUM in that he had a total lack of sympathy for women having any active voice or vote in the running of the miners' committees once the strike was over. Once back at work the miners often faced humiliating conditions down the pits, where men were in many ways made to pay the penalty for having been on strike. 'I'd change places every day and stay at home to look after the family if they'd pay me the same money,' said Phil. 'When women stopped working down the mines, they were the lucky ones.'

So, as women wept and begged men not to go back to work and to keep the strike going, it was not surprising that the miners reflected bitterly that at least the women did not have to go back underground on the unrelenting shift work. They could not see that for the women, too, it meant the end of dreams and hopes and a return to a life that they had, for the most part, found depressing and inadequate.

The women's movement which evolved during the strike regenerated pride among all working-class women. Their feminism was based not on a doctrine of individual opportunity, but on the strength of the solidarity of women to achieve a better and fairer society.

After the strike, the women had realised that the qualities they had been using in their fight to keep the pits open had previously been wasted. They concluded that if those qualities had not been held in such low esteem, if they themselves had been more in control of their own lives, the nightmare of the pit closures and nuclear power, together with a future on the dole, might never have happened. Their voices would have been heard.

It is possible to see these happenings simply in terms of working-class women adopting roles that other women already took for granted. But the miners' wives wanted to use their new-found freedom to change society and to improve it, just as they had used it to fight against pit closures. Since the strike they have already given money to many of those who supported them on the picket lines – nurses, the unemployed, printers at Wapping, CND supporters, students and refugees.

The women have seen that change must be political. For some, the way lay through ensuring that the Labour Party would be returned to power at the next General Election, and, indeed, many of the women's support groups moved closer to the Labour movement after the strike.

By 1986, the nuclear power programme was expanding rapidly. Meanwhile, the anti-nuclear movement became stronger, spurred on by the disaster at the Russian plant at Chernobyl, near Kiev which drew Europeans' attention to the lethal aspects of radiation. Greenham women were being proved right in their beliefs. The anti-nuclear movement, which many of the miners' wives have joined, has given strength and experience to the local organisations anxious about the post-Chernobyl, near Kiev, which drew Europeans' attention to the harmful effects of low-level radiation on their children and the possibilities of nuclear accidents.

There are many, too, who have become school governors, party political activists, leaders of projects for the Third World, and are all the time keeping to their promise to support those who supported them during the strike.

The impact on our society as a whole is not immediate or dramatic, but it is as powerful as the strength of women's solidarity which first flickered at Greenham Common and then spread throughout the country. With the 1984–85 coal strike a working-class based women's movement has been clearly defined. Women's proper contribution to the way the world is run will spring only from the solidarity of working-class women throughout the world.

Colliery Closures 1985–87

Note: This list does not include partial closures or mergers.

1985/86 (27 mines closed)

SOUTH WALES	Bedwas	Closed 31. 8.1985
	Celynen South	Closed 6. 9.1985
	Markham	Closed 20. 9.1985
	Treforgan	Closed 30. 9.1985
	Penrikyber	Closed 8.10.1985
	Abertillery	Closed -9.10.1985
	Aberpergwn	Closed 7.10.1985
	St John's	Closed 22.11.1985
	Garw	Closed 13.12.1985
NORTH EAST	Brenkley	Closed 25.10.1985
	Sacriston	Closed 15.11.1985
	Herrington	Closed 22.11.1985
	Horden	Closed 28. 2.1986
	Bates	Closed 25. 2.1986
NORTH YORKS	Ackton Hall	Closed 5. 7.1985
	Savile	Closed 28. 8.1985
	Fryston	Closed 6.12.1985
	Glasshoughton	Closed 28. 3.1985
SOUTH YORKS	Yorkshire Main	Closed 11.10.1985
	Brookhouse	Closed 25.10.1985
	Cortonwood	Closed 25.10.1985

BARNSLEY	Emley Moor	Closed 20.12.1985
WESTERN	Wolstanton	Closed 18.10.1985
	Haig	Closed 26.11.1985
	Bold	Closed 15.11.1985
SOUTH NOTTS	Moorgreen	Closed 19. 7.1985
	Pye Hill	Closed 9. 8.1985

1986/87 (14 mines closed)

SCOTTISH	Comrie	Closed 19. 9.1986
	Polkemmet	Closed 10. 6.1986
NORTH DERBY	Whitwell	Closed 27. 6.1986
SOUTH MIDS	Whitwick	Closed 4. 7.1986
	Birch Coppice	Closed 28.11.1986
NORTH YORKS	Kinsley Drift	Closed 11. 7.1986
	Ledston Luck	Closed 31.10.1986
SOUTH YORKS	Cadeby	Closed 7.11.1986
KENT	Tilmanstone	Closed 24.10.1986
NOTTS	Hucknall/Babbington	Closed 31.10.1986
SOUTH WALES	Nantgarw	Closed 7.11.1986
	Cwm	Closed 28.11.1986
WESTERN	Bersham	Closed 12.12.1986
NORTH EAST	Whittle	Closed 9. 1.1987

According to British Coal, on 9 March 1985 there were 172,363 mineworkers on the colliery books. On 14 February 1987 there were 114,974.

Index

Alderson, John, 61
Allen, Professor Vic, 26, 27
Anderson, Florence, 29, 115, 116, 117, 119, 124
Anderson, Margaret, 98

Barnsley Panel, 147
Barnsley rally and march, ix, x, 11, 18–21
    and Nottinghamshire women, 107
    size of, 19, 109
Barnsley Women Against Pit Closures, ix, x, xi, xiv, 14, 18, 59, 123
    and split, xii, 146–8
Bell, Philip, 122
Benn, Tony, xii, 16, 29, 30, 40, 85
Bennett, Kate, 130, 131, 133
Blidworth Women's Support Group, 15, 16
Bolton, George, 152
Boulton, Lesley, 134
Bowen, Kay, 36, 38
Bowen, Phil, 155, 166, 167
Bowler, Lorraine, 19
Britain and nuclear power, 1
British Coal, see National Coal Board

British Nuclear Fuels Limited, 7
bulk buying, 100

Cammell Laird shipyard, 77–8
Campaign for Nuclear Disarmament (CND), x, 48, 55, 168
Capenhurst nuclear processing plant, 108
Chernobyl, 7, 8, 165, 168
Chesterfield support group, 29, 45, 137, 149
Chesterfield Women's Conference, 21
children and problems with, 164
Christmas 1984, 148–50
Christmas Appeal, xiii, 137–9
chronology of the strike, xi–xiv
Clegg, Lynn, 11, 32, 34, 56, 64, 66, 166
Clegg, Tony, 32, 66
Clipstone Ladies Support Group, 50
Clipstone Soup Kitchen, 97–100
Coal Mines Bill 1911, 112
cold in winter, 37, 51, 71, 73, 77, 141, 142–4, 145
collieries
    Aberpergwn, 169
    Abertillery, 169

171

Ackton Hall, 169
Armthorpe, 33, 62, 65, 67–8
Bates, 169
Bedwas, 169
Bersham, 170
Bilston Glen, 5, 34, 35, 36, 149, 157, 162, 163
Birch Coppice, 170
Blaenant, 37, 38, 155, 166
Blidworth, 24, 39, 40, 42, 50, 97, 100–01, 104
Bold, 170
Brenkley, 169
Brookhouse, 170
Bullcliffe Wood, 153
Cadeby, 170
Calverton, 65, 66, 97
Cardowan, 3, 5
Celynen South, 169
Clipstone, 50, 97, 98, 100, 105, 155, 160
Comrie, 170
Cortonwood, ix, xii, 10, 100, 153, 170
Cwm, 122, 170
Easington, 117, 118, 151
Emley Moor, 76–7, 160, 170
Eppleton, 117, 124, 125, 126
Fryston, 169
Frances, 160
Garw, 169
Glasshoughton, 169
Grimethorpe, ix, xii, xiii, 68
Haig, 170
Haleswood, 113
Hatfield Main, xi, 11, 12, 33, 34, 56, 61–2, 64, 65, 70
Herrington, 153, 169
Horden, 169
Hucknall/Babbington, 97, 170
Kinsley Drift, 170
Ledston Luck, 170
Lewis Merthyr, 12
Maerdy, 39, 46, 64, 79–90, 157, 158, 165

Markham, 169
Monktonhall, 5, 34, 71–5, 154, 161
Moorgreen, 170
Murton, 118, 120, 122, 126
Nantgarw, 170
Ollerton, ix, 23, 62, 63, 65, 97, 102
Penrikyber, 169
Polkemmet, 5, 75–6, 170
Polmaise, ix, 2, 3, 4, 5, 10, 32, 33, 56, 150, 153, 154
Pye Hill, 170
Rainworth, 97
Sacriston, 169
St John's, 169
Savile, 169
Shirebrook, 101
Silverhill, x, 59
Silverwood, 70
Snowdown, 92, 153
South Elmsall, 65
Staverley, 59, 62
Tilmanstone, 170
Treforgan, 169
Upton, 65
Whittle, 170
Whitwell, 170
Whitwick, 170
Wolstanton, 170
Yorkshire Main, xii, 170
Conservative Government 1983–, 1, 8, 83, 89, 93
and anti-trade union laws, 61
and fear of NUM, 1
Conservative Party, the, 47
Coutts, Joyce, 34, 35
cruise missiles, 55, 58
Cummings, Alan, 117

Daily Mirror, 137, 138
Department of Health and Social Security (DHSS)
allowances, 127
laws, 11

Derbyshire Miners' Association, 112

Derbyshire Women's Action Group, 145–6

Douglas, Dave, 56

Douglass, Maureen, 19

Duncan, Isabel, 98

Edinburgh Gala, 47–9

EEPTU, 32

end of the strike, xiii, 135, 153–9

'enemies within', 5

Eppleton Area Miners' Wives' Support Group, 29, 116, 124–6, 161

European Community and nuclear power, 1

Evans, Glynnis, 64, 85, 86, 87

Evans, John, 64, 87

family divisions, 105–07, 111

family upheavals, 32, 42–6

February appeal, xiii, 139–40

fight for jobs, 6, 10, 13, 79, 109–11, 115

fight for the future, 109–11

fight from the grassroots, 2, 6

food parcels, 28, 31, 36–8, 40, 98–90, 92, 101, 124, 128, 131, 144, 145

fund raising, 4, 20, 24, 31, 32–3, 38, 42, 62, 85, 92, 99, 130–40, 146, 162, 164, 167

Gillespie, Robert, 143

Glasgow rally, 151–2

Grangemouth docks, 4, 33

Greater London Council (GLC), 100

Green, Joe, x, 154

green movement, the, 25

Greenham Common Peace Camp, xi, xii, 7, 14, 22, 47–58, 87, 159, 165, 168

Greenham women, xii, 20, 47–58,
85, 87, 131, 159, 168

and confidence, 51–2

and co-operation with mining women, 51, 54

and influence in Welsh coalfield, 57

and influence on mining women, 48

and miners, 47, 54–7

and prison reform, 58

and support given to mining communities, 49–52

and tactics of, 52

and unemployment, 58

and WAPC, 58

Greens Party, 8

Greenwood, Brenda, xiii, 62–3

Guardian, 67, 68, 100, 137, 138, 154

Hamilton, David, 157, 162

Hatfield Main Women's Support Group, 56

Hathaway, Lyn, 59

Hearst, David, 68

Heathfield, Betty, 21, 28, 40, 42, 62, 134, 146

Heathfield, Peter, xii, 40, 146

Hipperson, Sarah, 52

Hogg, Peter, 162

Hollis, Liz, 59

Holness, Jane, 98

Holroyd, Annette, 19

Humber, Doreen, 16, 40, 53, 108, 109

Industrial Relations Tribunals, 35, 164

injustices in pit villages, 50, 52, 56, 105, 161, 162–3

International Women's Day rally at Chesterfield, xiv

Irish Republican Army (IRA), 68

Jefferies, Claudia, 98

'jobs with peace', 48
Jones, David, xi, 62, 154
Jones, Kath, 17, 18

Kent, Bruce, x, 48
Kent coalfields, 79, 90–4
Kent miners, 159
  and militancy, 90
  and solidarity, 90
Kent Women's Support Groups,
  24, 92, 130, 131
King, Linda, 23, 102, 103
King, Rachel, 103, 104
Kinnock, Glenys, 57
Kinnock, Neil, 16, 85

Labour Party, the, 24–5, 29, 100,
  119, 168
  National Executive, 25
  women's representation within,
  25
lack of food, 144–5
Lilburn, Ann, 163, 164
Links organisation, 7, 165
London East End communities
  destruction of, 17–18
London march (June 1984), x
London march and rally (August
  1984), xi, 4, 21, 62, 132–3, 136
London rally (February 1985),
  xiii
Lothian Women's Committee, 34
Lowe, Elsie, 98, 99, 155
Lowe, John, 98, 99, 105, 160, 161
low-level radiation, 168
Lynk, Roy, 95–6

MacCormack, John, 2, 5, 10, 56
McCrindle, Jean, x, 113, 149
McGahey, Mick, 75, 123, 152,
  156
MacGregor, Sir Ian, xi, xii, 5, 6,
  81, 89, 129, 161

Maerdy Women's Support
  Group, 83, 85, 90
malnutrition, 50, 99, 130, 143,
  144–5, 164
Mansfield march and rally, x, 99
market economy, 81
media and NUM reaction to,
  68–70
meetings between NUM and
  NCB, x, xi, xii, xiii, 151–2, 157
Militancy of British Miners, The,
  26–7
militant pits, 79–94, 162
Miller, Jean, 14, 19, 20
miners
  and lack of solidarity after
    strike, 161
  and lack of understanding of
    Greenham women, 54–7
  and passive resistance, 55–7
  arrested, x, xi, xii, 50, 52, 61,
    74, 75, 103, 105, 162
  debts, 37, 164
  injured, 50, 55–6, 162
  imprisoned, 61, 84, 85, 162, 164
  killed, 162
  numbers of, 1, 170
  sacked, xiii, xiv, 35, 44, 75, 84,
    90, 92, 111, 119, 153, 155, 158,
    160, 161, 162, 163, 164
  violence to, 56, 162
  visits to Greenham, 52
miners' strike 1926, 29, 84, 85, 90,
  95
  and lock out, 95
miners' strike 1972, 10
miners' strike 1974, 10
'mines not missiles' rally, xii
mining children and militancy,
  87–8
mining communities
  and isolation, 12
  and lack of solidarity, 106
  and the media, 158–9
  and solidarity, 13
  under siege, 104–5

mining women
and allegiance to mining communities, 11, 12
and awareness of nuclear threat, 53
and depression, 128
and education, 11, 13–15, 33
and exploitation of, 25–28, 85–6, 115–22
and feminism, 9, 20, 33
and friendship, 164
and independence, 32
and international politics, 7, 22–4, 165
and knowledge of coal mining, 11
and Labour Party, 24–5
and lack of consultation with, 154–5
and leading marches back to work, 156–7, 158
and links with other industries, 77–8
and male domination by, 13–14, 41, 115–22
and minority groups, 107–08
and NUM, 113–24, 134
and picketing, 59–78, 120–1, 124, 147, 159
and police violence towards, 62–7, 102–4
and politicisation of, 7, 11, 24, 39, 46, 84, 88, 119
and sexual harassment, 64
and social life, 40–2
and solidarity, 35, 164
and strength of support for strike, 10
and ties to shift work, 165–6
and trade unions, 13–14
and traditional roles, 39
and visits to Greenham, 52–4
against return to work, 155
arrested, x, xi, 11, 59, 62–4, 65–6, 104

as 'the walking wounded', 126–9
modernisation of pits, 6, 49, 83
monetarist policies, 1, 23, 81
Monktonhall Women's Support Committee, 151, 154
Moore, Audrey, 59
Moore, Nellie, 98
Murton Wives' Support Group, 118, 156

National Coal Board (NCB), ix, xi, xiii, 1, 3, 4, 5, 11, 35, 44, 67, 71, 75, 76, 79, 81, 92, 97, 98, 100, 105, 125, 139, 140, 142, 153, 160, 161, 162, 163, 164
and helpful attitude to media, 68
and sacking miners, 75
back to work bonuses, xii, 67, 101, 139, 151
backlash, 138–9
propaganda, 101–02
National Union of Mineworkers (NUM), xii, 7, 11, 12, 21, 22, 24, 34, 47, 61, 69, 70, 75, 76, 88, 90, 92, 93, 99, 104, 112, 113, 115, 116, 117, 119, 120, 122, 123, 130, 134, 135, 136, 139, 146, 147, 151, 155, 157, 160, 165, 167
and mining women, 113–24, 134
as bastion of male chauvinism, 119
associate membership for women, x, 113–24
attitudes to journalists, 5, 68–70
delegate conference (March 1985), xii, 153, 156, 157
executive, ix, xii, 2, 5, 70, 115, 162
funds, xii

opposition to government, 1
support from other unions, 60
winding down the strike, 70
National Union of Public Em-
    ployees (NUPE), 77, 117
National Women's Organisation,
    21
Neale, Barbara, 98
Newman, Kenneth, 60
North Yorkshire Women Against
    Pit Closures, 127
Northern College, Barnsley, xi,
    xiii, 17
    Conference, summer 1984, 14
'Not just tea and sandwiches'
    exhibition, 133–4
Nottinghamshire and District
    Miners' Industrial Union, 95
Nottinghamshire Central
    Women's Support Group, 59,
    97
Nottinghamshire Miners' Asso-
    ciation, 95
Nottinghamshire striking miners'
    wives, 96–111
    and isolation, 96–97
Nottinghamshire Women's Sup-
    port Groups, 108
nuclear power, 1, 6, 7, 22, 27,
    47–58, 108, 165, 167
    and pollution, 8, 49

Ollerton Colliery Women's Sup-
    port Group, 23
Orgreave coking plant, x, 69, 136

Parry, Johnnie, 156
Parry, Mary, 118, 156
passive resistance, 31, 54, 55–57
*People's History of Yorkshire No.
    12*, xiv
Petney, Susan, 15, 24, 40, 109
picketing, x, xi, xii, xiv, 31, 42,
    46, 56, 59–78, 94, 99, 116, 124,
    125, 146, 151, 159

pit closures, 160, 161, 169–70
pit transfer systems, 18
pneumoconiosis (miner's lung),
    81, 83, 86
police and helpful attitudes to
    media, 68
    tactics on picket lines, 60–1, 93
    violence, 56, 60, 61, 62, 64, 65,
    66, 67, 68, 69, 70, 93, 102–05
    weaponry, 61
Potter, Carole, 98
public speaking, 4, 15–17, 31, 32,
    38, 42, 44, 46, 86, 88, 119, 132

Radford, Pauline, 15, 16, 39, 42
Ravenscraig steel works, x, 56,
    136
Red Mary of the Rhondda, 84
redundancies, ix, 6, 92, 160, 161
redundancy payments, 5
return to work, 155–7
Rhondda valleys, 81, 82, 86, 88
role reversals, 31, 39–42, 117
Royal   Ulster   Constabulary
    (RUC), 60, 68

Save Easington Area Mines
    Group, 118–19
scabs, 36, 37, 38, 62, 63, 65, 71,
    74, 89, 101, 102, 103, 106, 107,
    111, 125, 146, 148, 154, 158,
    161
Scargill, Anne, x, 59, 134, 147
Scargill, Arthur, x, xii, 2, 6, 19,
    20, 68, 69, 107, 122, 126, 147,
    154
    and leadership, 96
scratting for coal, 84, 141
Smillie, Robert, 113
Social Democratic Party (SDP),
    15
Socialist Action, 18
soup kitchens, 3, 4, 18, 28, 29, 31,
    33–6, 43, 44, 60, 93, 97, 98,
    100, 101, 103, 115, 116, 124,

128, 134, 145, 166
South Wales coalfield, 157
Spencer, George, 95
'Spencerism', 95
Strike 84–85 booklet, 126–29
strike
  chronology of, ix-xiv
Striking Women 63
strip searches, 63–4
Suddick, Anne, 165
Sunday Times, x, 32, 115
support from the public, 70, 130–40
support groups, 17–18, 31, 34
  and continuation after strike, 166
Sutcliffe, Kay, 24, 54, 64, 92, 93
Sutcliffe, Philip, 92
Swain, John, 154

Taylor, Jack, 19
Thatcher, Margaret, 1, 5, 6, 15, 68, 89, 101, 104, 126, 129, 152
trade union support, 135–7
Trades Union Congress (TUC), 14, 25, 135
Transport and General Workers' Union (TGWU), 132, 136
Triple Alliance, 136
Torness nuclear power station, 48–9

unemployment, xi, 6, 10–11, 13, 17, 35, 45, 58, 74, 76, 81, 83, 111, 137, 138, 140, 151
Union of Democratic Mineworkers, 96

voucher systems, 4, 34
violence on picket lines, 56, 60–70, 93, 102–5, 135

Wainwright, Hilary, 138
Wheeler, Albert, 2
Whiteside, Kate, 29, 30, 45, 149
Williams, Babs, 46, 85, 90, 157, 165
Williamson, Alfreda, 120, 121, 122
Windsor, Roger, 24
Wintour, Patrick, 154
women and the vote, 9
Women Against Pit Closures (WAPC), xii, 7, 8, 20, 21–2, 61, 62, 108. 109, 112, 115, 148, 163, 164, 165
  aims, 22
  and Greenham women, 58
  and London rally and march (August 1984), xi, 4, 21, 62, 132–3, 136
  and nuclear power, 8
women as cheap labour, 26–7, 81
women in prison, 49
'Women for mines not missiles', 108
Women for Peace, 108
women miners in USA, 112
women working in the pits, 112–3
Wood, Heather, 118
working-class women's movement, 20, 27–30, 31, 46, 167–8
working-class wife, myth of, 28

Yorkshire Area Women Against Pit Closures, xiii
Young Communist League, 14
Younger, George, 152
Youth Training Schemes, 83, 84